How To Make A Miracle

By
Margaret Pounders

Copyright © 2013 Margaret Pounders

All rights reserved.

ISBN: 0988414104

ISBN 13:   9780988414105

Library of Congress Control Number: 2012919337

CreateSpace Independent Publishing Platform,
North Charleston, SC

Contents

You - Miracle Maker v

Chapter I: *Understanding The Mystic Code* 1

Chapter II: *The First Law – Faith* 27

Chapter III: *The Second Law – Commitment* 55

Chapter IV: *The Third Law – Relaxation*........................79

Chapter V: *The Fourth Law – Imagination* 105

Chapter VI: *The Fifth Law – The Power
Of The Word*..133

Chapter VII: *The Sixth Law – Thanksgiving*................167

Chapter VIII: *The Seventh Law – Forgiveness* 191

Chapter IX: *The Miracle Model* 217

Chapter X: *As Above, So Below* 241

You – Miracle Maker

> "Truly, truly, I say to you, he who believes in me will also do the works that I do; and greater works than these will he do . . ."
>
> – Jesus (John 13:12).

Miracles happen every day. Every time a goal is set and achieved, a miracle takes place. The fact is that every event in our life is a miracle, because each happening is an aspiration attained, whether consciously or unconsciously desired or not desired.

Some persons are fearful of the concept of miracles, believing them to be ignorant superstition or terrifyingly supernatural. Miracles have nothing to do with superstition. They are, however, supernatural, because they follow certain Spiritual laws – laws that reach beyond the physical to the metaphysical and are reliable and repeatable.

Miracle-making is an orderly process, always following a certain sequence of events. First, an idea is conceived in mind, then accepted by the conscious phase of mind as a possibility and nurtured with emotion by the feeling nature – perhaps with joy, perhaps fear. We see the end result, and we name it good or bad. We feel a sense of joyous expectation, or perhaps we worry. Then we talk about it, providing energy to plant that seed within the soil of the mind where it never fails to grow.

Inevitably, that seed idea becomes a reality in our experience, whether wanted or not. (In later chapters, we will examine the process through which this seed idea is planted and grows.) Strangely enough, most of us never realize we have any control over this process, believing instead that things simply happen to us.

There are certain steps taken each time a miracle is demonstrated, and fortunately, the keys to making the miracle we choose are laid out in a book readily available to all. We call it the "Bible." Many of our first introductions to the Bible were fearsome tales, smoldering with fire and brimstone, a book whose covers were best left unopened. Many continue to feel that way even into adulthood. This is superstition, and it is unfortunate for us if we hold such beliefs. The Bible is not a book to be feared, but to be mastered. It is the story of your life – what you have been, what you are becoming and what you are destined to be.

Just imagine a beautiful book given to you, and emblazoned in gold letters on the cover are the words, "THIS IS THE LIFE OF..." followed by your name. Would that not arouse your curiosity? Of course it would. And as you opened that very first page and began to read about your origins and how they influence you today, you would begin to understand where many of your fears and negative feelings came from. You would also discover how some of its truest values became a part of your life. On the human level alone, you would certainly gain a greater understanding of your own parents and family members, and perhaps even forgive and love them a bit more.

We read in the Old Testament, "The Lord is slow to anger and abounding in steadfast love, forgiving iniquity and transgression, but he will by no means clear the guilty, visiting the iniquity of fathers upon children, upon the third and upon the fourth generation" (Numbers 14:18).

This is, most likely, one of the statements of scripture that drive people away from the Bible. Too bad we tend to ignore the first part of the sentence, while latching onto the last. In actual fact, it is a simple statement of the far-reaching effects of the law of cause and effect or mind action. It is important that we realize that this is not the expression of God, but of the law as people several thousand years ago interpreted it.

All things that happened to these ancient people were attributed to Yahweh, their tribal God. If disaster struck, they had somehow displeased Yahweh and this was their punishment. When they prospered, it was because Yahweh was once again pleased.

The writer of the book of Numbers was doubtlessly conservative in stating that actions last three or four generations. Today we see how certain behaviors, such as child abuse, alcoholism and drug addiction (to name only a few) pass on to future generations. The abused child becomes the abuser of his or her own children and perhaps even grandchildren. The abuser, as well as the abused, almost never regains the feelings of self-worth necessary to live a really fulfilled life. How can he/she? This is not limited to physical abuse. The children of alcoholics and drug abusers also face long-term psychological pain and trauma.

To state that the errors and mistakes of our forebears pass down to us for three or four generations is conservative. They may very likely pass down for ten or twelve generations in ways we do not fully understand. Surely all of us have seen this. But with our God-given freedom of choice, we have the power to change those attributes we have accepted as unchangeable, and choose lives that bless ourselves and those who come after us. Remind yourself, "Just because Mama did it, it ain't necessarily right!"

But it works both ways. The right thinking and right action of our parents, grandparents and even great grandparents also pass down to us, and we bless and give thanks for their gifts.

As you read the story of your beginnings in the Old Testament, you realize that these forebears of yours had very primitive concepts regarding God or Spirit, and you see how these erroneous doctrines continued. They influenced the children of those who believed them. These children, in turn, influenced their children to believe in a god who was wrathful and beyond human comprehension or communication. And so it continues. Factually, this god sometimes appears as one who does not really like his creation very much. Unfortunately, these interpretations remain with us today. There are people who will literally fight to maintain these false beliefs.

But as you read further in the Bible, you begin to see that an evolution takes place in our progenitors' thinking and belief systems. Change comes slowly, but it is discernible. Yet even their evolved beliefs are not ones you or I would feel comfortable with or care to adopt. They are still strange enough to bring fear to the hearts of many. Nevertheless, as we read the Old Testament chronologically, we begin to sense that their god is showing at least some compassion to a favored few, though still demanding constant praise and adulation for himself.

(No offense, Gentlemen, but the fact is that this early concept of god was decidedly masculine.)

Becoming a Bible scholar or even reading every word of the Bible is not necessary to understanding this book. All you need do is understand that the portion marked Old Testament, with its scary stories, as well as its beautiful poetry and wisdom literature, is the story of the evolution of humankind's *understanding* of God; not the story of God and a favored few.

Metaphysical interpretation will be offered as we go along. *Metaphysics* simply means *spiritual* or above the *physical*. As we read the events of the Gospels together, keep in mind that, even though this was not the god of whom Jesus taught, Jesus was dealing with people who still saw their god in a very primitive light. It was Jesus' custom to work with them from their current position in consciousness, rather than to force his wisdom upon them.

In the four Gospels of the Master Teacher, we really begin to learn about ourselves and discover the pattern for making our own lives unending miracles.

We see Jesus, our Example, and know that we personally are destined to express our own unique Christ consciousness, just as he did. This is the ultimate. But along the way, as we study his life, we see the various places he passed through and we know that these are our states of consciousness on our personal Spiritual journey. We meet people with no insight (blind) and those who possess unclean thoughts (lepers). We pass through periods of intense decision-making (the wilderness) and areas of confusion (Samaria). We rise to a high level of spiritual awareness (the Mount of Transfiguration or any mountain or high place) and continue to seek that state of perfect peace (Jerusalem). We realize that we, too, have dwelt in each of these places at one time or another.

We begin to know that we really are the heroes and heroines of this marvelous book of life.

We see, too, that we are being taught how to overcome challenges and improve our lives right here on earth, all the while moving toward the expression of our own Christhood, as Jesus did.

As children, many of you, like me, may have been taught that the miracles of Jesus were acts out of the norm, to be accepted with blind faith, performed for the purpose of proving that Jesus was different from the rest of humankind.

One Bible commentary I read states that the credibility of the New Testament miracle depends on this very element of difference between Jesus and ourselves.

Perhaps you find this theory unsatisfactory. I do. It was this very implied difference between Jesus and the rest of us that made it difficult for me to relate to him or find a teaching which allowed me to fully appreciate Jesus and his miracles. I am grateful that I found that teaching.

Jesus was a practical man. Never did he perform tricks for the entertainment or adulation of the crowds. Nor did he have any desire to be viewed as different. He experienced those temptations in the wilderness and rejected them (Matthew 4:5-10). Jesus' statement was, "Truly, truly I say to you, he who believes in me will also do the works that I do; and greater works than these will he do..." (John 14:12).

"He who believes in me..." – he who recognizes his own Christ-potential and follows the example of Jesus.

We might look at the miracles performed by Jesus in the Gospels as another method by which he taught and emphasized his teachings. Precepts and parables could be misunderstood. Even his actions were and still are open to question. Jesus' own disciples frequently failed to grasp his deeper teachings.

Jesus recognized that the Truth he was offering must be presented in a way that could, first, get attention, and second, not be misinterpreted. As a result, we may consider the recorded miracles of Jesus as another way in which he taught Spiritual law in a practical and constructive manner and in a way that gained and held people's attention. His purpose was to make these higher teachings evident and available to everyone.

A miracle then, is not taking place outside our scientific laws of physics; it is not superstition nor is it magic, but, rather the outworking of laws that are understandable and repeatable. Many of these are not yet understood by the majority of people, yet they remain available to all. When we comprehend them, we can perform them and repeat them.

And so we see that the Gospels are the story of each one of us and our multitude of experiences on our way to Christhood – the characters we meet, the events we undergo, the places we travel... And Jesus represents that perfect pattern for us to emulate, the Christ Model that God knows each of us to be.

When the idea for this book first came to me, more than ten years ago, it was my intent to take each of Jesus' miracles, examine it individually, then interpret the steps he used in that particular event. However, as I studied and meditated on his healing miracles, a model emerged. The most obvious step in that model was faith. In every miracle the use of faith was either spoken or implied.

As I continued to study the healing miracles, it seemed more helpful to examine these steps than the individual miracle, itself. Interestingly enough, the parts, when joined together, formed a pattern: faith; commitment; a relaxed state of mind; the ability to see the desired outcome in advance of its happening (imagination or visualization); speaking the word of Truth (affirmations and denials); and giving thanks in advance for the answered prayer. Each of these is essential. And in some instances, though not all, Jesus indicated that forgiveness was needed.

As I analyzed Jesus' other miracles – those referred to as miracles of nature, supply and overcoming death – the pattern remained the same. As a result, I continued studying these individual steps to determine if they could be used to overcome any challenge or to ensure the success of every opportunity. I believe they can.

In this book a variety of Jesus' miracles will be used to illustrate his use of the miracle model. The same miracle may sometimes be used more than once to emphasize various aspects which brought it into being.

Do not read hurriedly. Jesus performed instantaneous miracles, and that is not out of the realm of possibility.

Most of us, however, have spent a lifetime learning to doubt ourselves and God. The human consciousness has been well-trained in beliefs regarding lack and limitations. We have worked hard at learning to disbelieve that the dreams dearest our hearts could become a reality. Many of us actually feel unloving and unloved by God and humankind. As a result, we may need to learn to crawl before we walk or run. Remember that Jesus told us "Whoever does not receive the kingdom of God like a child shall not enter it" (Mark 10:15).

Never forget that you are reading the story of YOUR life: the story of the evolution in humankind's thinking about Who and What God is, as well as the experiences you personally pass through on your way to becoming the One you are destined to be.

God blesses you on this journey.

Chapter 1

Understanding The Mystic Code

"For it is written that Abraham had two sons, one by a slave and one by a free woman... Now this is an allegory; these women are two covenants..."

(GALATIANS 4:21-24)

"With many such parables he (Jesus) spoke the word to them, as they were able to hear it: he did not speak to them without a parable, but privately to his own disciples he explained everything" (Mark 4:33, 34).

You are the Bible incarnate. The Bible is your personal life story. Within you is every character, every place, every situation. At one time or another, you have played every role.

The Bible is the story of our lives from Genesis to spiritual ascension. In the Bible we discover not only what we *are*, but what we are destined to *become*, for it is within the mind, the consciousness, that we house these myriad performances.

In this ancient and mystical book we discover how we can make our lives the successful, exciting experience that a life should be; we find the clues to why we have fallen short of that goal; we find the secrets to making our miracle.

A Secret Code

In order to follow the directions given in this book of life, it is necessary to break what may seem to be a mystical code. To break simply means to break it down into its component parts in order to understand its deeper meanings. This code is logical, however, and with a little persistence can be understood by anyone, as it has been by seekers for thousands of years.

When I first began my personal study of the Bible as a practical guide and not merely an object to be revered, I read many books and attended many lectures. Some were helpful; some were not. Among the most valuable to my research were those published by Unity School of Christianity, especially THE METAPHYSICAL BIBLE

DICTIONARY and *THE REVEALING WORD*. I highly recommend them as resources for every serious student of metaphysics.

Very briefly, here are some of the keys that help to unlock the mystical language of the Bible and all allegorical literature, as well as your personal nightly dreams.

Names of people and places are among the most important aspects of metaphorical symbolism. A name describes the nature of the one to whom it refers. To the Hebrews, names were of utmost importance, and naming a child or a place was to proclaim the child's character. "He leads me in the paths of righteousness for his name's sake" (Psalm 23:3).

Let us examine a few names to illustrate how this type of interpretation can be applied. Joshua was the leader of Moses' army and the one who led the Israelites into Canaan after Moses' death. In Hebrew the name *Joshua* appropriately means *Jehovah is salvation; Jehovah is deliverer; Jehovah is the victory. Joshua* is the Hebrew form of the Greek, *Jesus.* Obviously, this name would signify *a highly spiritual personage,* which Joshua does indeed represent.

Now compare this to the meaning of *Antipas*, the given name of the Judean King Herod, generally regarded as the beheader of John the Baptist. In Greek, Antipas means *against one's native country; against all.*

By the simple translation of these names to their original language, we see that two very different types of human nature are represented.

Unfortunately, interpretation of names is not always so obvious. Two persons with the same name may represent conflicting traits. For example, the Hebrew name *Judah* literally means *praise Jehovah: celebration of Jehovah; laud Jehovah*. In the Old Testament Judah was the fourth son of Jacob and Leah, the father of the tribe from which the nation of Judea was formed. He was also an ancestor of Jesus. Clearly, this name indicates a *commendable aspect of character*, generally considered to be *prayer* and *praise*.

The Greek form of the Hebrew Judah is Judas, the name of the disciple who betrayed Jesus. While there are many conflicting theories as to his motive in doing this, he is not generally seen as so laudable a personage.

For purposes of interpretation we can see that in addition to the literal meaning of the name, the context of the story must always be considered.

States Of Mind

Names of places refer to states of mind. The city on a mountain, *Jerusalem,* in Hebrew means *habitation of peace;*

dwelling place of peace, possession of peace, while *Babylon,* the Greek form of the Hebrew, *Babel,* refers to *confusion; chaos; vanity; nothingness.*

Suppose I were to tell you, "I feel as though I'm living in Babylon today," you would understand that I am experiencing a time of confusion. If, on the other hand, I were to say, "I feel as though I'm on a mountain in Jerusalem," you would be much more likely to seek my company. Two totally different states of mind are indicated by the names of these places. But again, we must be aware of the context of the story in which the name appears. To a Babylonian, my statements would mean the opposite than to a Jew. As we interpret the Bible, we take the position of the Jew.

Certain words can be literally interpreted. *Mountains or high places* refer to *lofty states of consciousness,* while *valleys* signify *low* or *depressed conditions of mind,* ("... the valley of the shadow of death") (Psalms 23:4). A *lamb* symbolizes *innocence and guilelessness,* whereas *lion* stands for *fearlessness and courage,* perhaps even *aggressive initiative.*

Kings and *queens* or *any person in a position of leadership* signify *dominant phases of mind,* whereas *unnamed persons* generally represent *thoughts* and *feelings* that we might say *people the scene* of an event. In movies they would be called *extras.*

Numbers are significant in Biblical interpretation. The ancient Hebrews were immersed in numerology, and much of the meaning of Biblical allegory is summed up by the numbers used. Note, for example, the frequent use of the number *forty*. The flood from which Noah and his family were saved lasted forty days and nights (Genesis 7:12). Moses' life is divided into three periods of forty years each (Exodus): Jesus fasted forty days and forty nights in the wilderness (Matt. 4:2). The number *forty* is an *indeterminate length of time*. We might say, "It's however long it takes to get the job done."

Men And Women

Whether the character is a man or a woman is important. A *woman* refers to the *feeling nature,* while a *man* represents the *thinking nature*. This in no way implies that women do not think or that men do not feel. We are each a mixture of both thinking and feeling. This is simply part of the Bible's secret language.

The type of woman named determines the character of the feeling she represents. The difference may be designated by a word or by the name of the woman. The distinction between the feeling represented by a *harlot* and a *queen* is obvious, as is the distinction between

Jezebel, the heretic queen of Israel, *and Mary, the mother of Jesus,* to those who read of these ladies.

Similarly, the identity of the man in question presents different faces. By studying the context of their stories. *King Herod* would be a very different dominant state of consciousness than *King David.*

Jesus always represents the *eternal, Spirit part of each of us, our indwelling divinity,* the *Christ Principle* in humankind. Jesus lived this Christ Principle so completely and was so unified with it that there was no separation between the two: Jesus, the human being and Jesus, the Christ. This is the goal for each of us as well.

Jesus had studied allegorical writings since childhood and understood them thoroughly; thus, he taught in parables and acted them out as part of his teaching ministry. He was the Master Psychologist, one who had truly mastered the study of the human soul.

If we wished to become a truly excellent musician, it would be wise to study under one who had mastered music. The same is true of any art or craft. It is true in life, as well. How could we learn more about abundant living, about miracle-making, than from Jesus?

Let us begin this study by examining the story of the very first miracle performed by Jesus, then interpret its meaning in our lives by applying these symbols. The symbols are classic. They are ageless. By thoroughly understanding the interpretation of this one particular miracle, a serious student would probably be able to interpret most scripture, literature and mythology, as well as their own dreams and fantasies.

Wedding At Cana (John 2:1-11)

Jesus' first miracle took place at a wedding in Cana of Galilee, which he attended with his family and disciples. A high point of many of our wedding ceremonies today is reference to the fact that Jesus himself demonstrated approval of marriage by his own presence at a wedding feast. This is a very important miracle, for with it Jesus set the scene and provided a pattern for understanding interpretation and, even more important, his personal philosophy of life.

Cana of Galilee is a small town about four miles northeast of Jesus' hometown of Nazareth. The wedding feast that day was surely much different from those we attend, though by no means less festive. Far from it!

In Jesus' day, it was customary for a young man to be married at about eighteen years of age, while his bride may have been only twelve or thirteen years old. As in the early days of our own country, they generally married within the community in which they lived.

Marriage plans began when the young woman's father and her suitor's best man agreed on the dowry. At that time the betrothal was announced and celebrated by the groom's simple declaration, "She is my wife and I her husband, from today and forever." These words, witnessed by friends and family, legally bound the young couple.

The betrothal lasted about a year, and during this period the bride and groom continued to live with their families. Unlike our engagement periods of today, however, it was a legal, binding contract and the girl could not be put away except by an official letter of divorce. Should the young man die, she was given all the respect due a widow. According to the Gospels of Matthew and Luke, it was during this betrothal period of Joseph and Mary that Jesus' birth took place.

The narrator of this first miracle fails to tell us the names of the bride and groom at the wedding that took place that day in Cana, but through the marvelous power of our imaginations, we can move through time and space to attend this very special feast, the culmination of the couple's yearlong betrothal.

We first arrive at the home of the bride's parents where the air is filled with excitement and activity. We see the bride, clothed for the festivities in a crown and elaborate dress, surrounded by enthusiastic, chattering family and friends.

Soon the groom and his entourage arrive to take her by carriage to the house she will now share with her husband. As we follow the noisy procession, we notice members of the community excitedly pouring oil, wine and grains along the way to ensure the happiness and fertility of the young couple.

On arriving at their home, we listen as the parents offer their blessing, and the musicians begin to play. Vast amounts of food and drink are available, and eating, drinking and dancing begin in earnest. If this is a wealthy family, the feast may last a full week, but a celebration of at least two or three days is to be expected from those in even the most humble of circumstances.

Point Of Honor

This may seem overly lavish by today's standards, but to a Jewish family of Jesus' time, hospitality was a point of honor and a wedding feast was the most important of events.

But all is not well at this particular feast. Something is amiss. As we listen, we overhear an anxious conversation between the groom's mother and another woman, addressed as *Mary*. The groom's mother is embarrassed, for already the wine is running low.

Immediately, the woman called *Mary* hastens to the side of a strong young man. She addresses him as *Jesus, my son*, and explains the predicament, then asks him to take care of it. Surprisingly, he seems to ignore her, but undaunted, Mary tells the servants to follow his orders, whatever they might be.

As Jesus looks about, he sees six stone jars for the Jewish rite of purification waiting nearby, each jar capable of holding twenty or thirty gallons of liquid. Hurriedly, he instructs the servants to fill the jars with water; then draws out a portion to take to the steward of the feast.

Fascinated, we watch the steward's amazement as he tastes, not water, but the finest of wine! He then calls the bridegroom to him, proclaiming: "Every man serves the good wine first; and when men have drunk freely, the poor wine; but you have kept the good wine until now" (John 2:10).

More Than A Story

The story of the wedding feast at Cana is a pleasant tale with a happy ending, one that each of us can enjoy and relate to in our everyday lives. A wedding is an emotion-filled event.

Who of us has not attended a wedding and felt a lump in our throat at the strains of the wedding march? Who cannot imagine the embarrassment at inviting friends and family to such a happy occasion, only to have refreshments run short? Who cannot understand a mother's pride as she calls on her son, a prominent new rabbi in the area, and asks him to come forward to remedy the situation? Each of us has surely felt such emotions.

As with all events in the Bible, we know the happenings at that wedding in Cana are of more importance than a mere tale to be told to entertain or to prove Jesus' *difference from* the rest of humankind. Jesus was illustrating something very important about each of us.

Many of Jesus' parables, designed to teach our high potential for life, began with the words, "The kingdom of heaven is like…" Had Jesus told this as a story, he might have begun, "The kingdom of heaven is like a wedding feast."

Let us now examine this event and see what it means to us, individually.

The Cast Of Characters

The characters in our drama are Jesus, his disciples, his mother Mary, the servants, and the wedding steward. (Strangely enough, in the scriptural text, the bride is never mentioned and the bridegroom, barely, in passing.) We begin by acquainting ourselves with this cast.

First, there is Jesus. Spiritually, *Jesus* represents the *Christ; God expressing in each human being.* We might refer to the *Christ Principle* within each of us as the *only begotten son* (John 3:16), the *seed of* God, which is our personal and individual *Real Self,* our *Individuality.* This indwelling Spirit is birthless, deathless and unchanging. It is *Immanuel. "God in us"* (Matthew 1:23). This Christ is the way our Creator sees each of us. That is, just as he saw Jesus.

The *calling of the disciples* by Jesus symbolically refers to the *transformation* that takes place when *human nature merges with its spiritual nature.* Certain eastern philosophies teach that there are specific centers of spiritual power situated in a *subtle body* that permeates the physical body. In these philosophies, these centers are referred to as *chakras.*

To our western way of thinking and in accord with such western mystics and philosophers such as Charles Fillmore, the founder of Unity, we might consider *Jesus' disciples* as representing inner qualities or faculties that when spiritualized, when taught or quickened (enlivened), become *Spiritual Powers* to be used for great good. Jesus eventually called twelve disciples and each of them had important, individual functions.

From a spiritual point of view, the number *twelve* refers to *spiritual wholeness* or *completeness*. Mystics throughout the ages have understood the significance of the number *twelve*, and it was of particular importance to the Jewish people of Jesus' day. There were twelve months in the Jewish calendar and twelve signs of the zodiac, twelve stones in Aaron's breastplate, twelve spies sent by Moses into Canaan, twelve stones of which the altar was made, and especially twelve sons of Jacob, who became the twelve tribes of Israel.

As we consider the significance of the relationship of Jesus and his disciples we might think of *Jesus* as representing the *fully Christed Individual;* a human being functioning at his or her total spiritual capacity. The *twelve disciples* symbolize the *component parts of that totality;* just as the *twelve tribes of Israel* were component parts of the nation as a whole.

It is of particular significance to note that at the time of this first miracle, Jesus had not yet called all twelve of his disciples. Only *five* are accounted for. The number five is generally associated with the *five physical senses*.

We might say that Jesus had not yet totally identified himself with his full spiritual potential, but had control of his physical senses. This is very important, for it means that we need not wait until we reach perfection or total Christhood to perform seeming miracles in our own lives. We start right where we are.

The Human Soul

The next character in our drama is *Mary, the mother of Jesus.* She represents the *human soul.*

To understand the activity of the soul, we must understand something of our own nature. We are three-fold beings – body, soul and Spirit. Our body is not only a material organism with physical senses; it is also the temple that houses our soul and Spirit. The words *Spirit, Christ* and *Superconscious Mind* can be used interchangeably. They represent the perfect pattern of each of us in God-Mind. *Spirit* is that *eternal part* of us that *sees* and *knows only pure unadulterated Truth.*

Spirit and soul are not synonymous. Soul is the essence of everything we have ever thought, felt or experienced. The soul is in constant communication with our human selves, guiding us, guarding us, protecting us, ever leading us to greater and greater good. It is also in constant contact with Spirit. The *soul* is the *bridge between our humanity and divinity.* It receives Truth from Spirit, but is also aware of that which takes place on the sensate plane.

A function of the soul is beautifully illustrated in the story of the wedding feast. Recall that even before the servants had become aware that the wine was running low, Mary, who symbolizes the soul, knew and asked Jesus to correct the situation. Jesus, in turn, told the servants to fill the six available pots with water, draw some out and take it to the steward of the feast.

The *servants* represent those *elemental subjective forces that* carry out our automatic bodily processes. Among other things, they digest our food; they assimilate the oxygen from the air we breathe; they have responsibility for our motor functions without our ever taking conscious thought. Would it not be inconvenient to lay awake at night making certain that we breathe and digest our food?

The Wine Of Life

The spiritual interpretation of *wine* is *spiritualized life*, life vitalized beyond the commonplace. Again, let us look at this miracle as if it were taking place in your life or mine, with all the characters a part of us.

Mary, the soul, recognizes that the vitality of life is running low and she turns to the Christ in absolute faith that he can handle the challenge.

How often does this happen to us? How many healings do you suppose each of us has experienced without even being aware that something was out of order? The answer to this question will probably never be known, yet through autopsies performed on accident victims, there is evidence that a surprising number of spontaneous healings of so-called *incurable diseases* have taken place that were never diagnosed, much less medically treated. Similarly, how often do you suppose that order and harmony have been reestablished in relationships and financial affairs without our ever knowing that a challenge existed?

When we practice daily prayer and meditation, our souls are in contact with the Christ, our Spiritual Source, just as Mary was in contact with Jesus. Without this daily contact, however, we are literally bombarded by negative impressions through our physical senses, which, unless habitually denied, reproduce in our world in some way.

"It's flu season!" the television booms. "Recession!" the news commentator pronounces. "Times are hard!" friend tells friend, and the word spreads and noses run and money is hoarded, then dries up (the money, not the nose), because the thing that we accept – whether consciously or unconsciously – becomes a fact in our lives that must be dealt with. This is the *law of mind action* – thoughts held in mind produce after their kind. It is also known as the *law of cause and effect.*

But a time of quiet contemplation of Who and What we are and of our relationship to that Power which created the Universe removes these undesirables from our consciousness. There is no way we can possibly know how often prayer and meditation bring about healings and harmonizing before the conscious mind even has reason to suspect a need.

Most physicians and caregivers now stress the importance of meditation and prayer for physical and mental health. (If yours does not, find one who does, for he/she is far behind times in medical therapy.)

It may seem strange that Jesus at first seemed reluctant to carry out his mother's request. (We will examine this seeming hesitancy in a later chapter.) Nevertheless, Mary persisted and told the servants to follow his orders.

Even when it appears that our need is impossible to meet, we must proceed as Mary did. Mary had total faith in Jesus. We, too, must have faith that the innate Christ Principle within us can and will correct all inharmonious situations.

At the wedding feast in Cana, Jesus told the servants – our subjective inner forces – to take six pots and fill them with water. The *water pots, filled to the brim* with water, represent the *extent to which life is prepared to pour itself out to us* when we are receptive. The only limitation is the receptacle, our consciousness.

The water with which Jesus told the servants to fill the pots represents *natural, human life, unexpressed capacities and potentialities*. Water can take numerous forms – steam, ice, and as ice, its shape and form is limited only by the mold which holds it. In this desert land, where water was scarce, it was truly a miracle that the water continued to flow until the pots were filled to the brim, just as the widow's meal and oil continued to multiply itself in the story of Elijah and the widow.

Metaphysically, *wine* signifies the *spiritualized, vitalized, fulfilled life as* "...wine to gladden the heart of man," wrote the Psalmist (Psalm 104:15).

This transmutation of water into wine takes place in our lives when we remind ourselves of Who and What we really are and realize our oneness with this indwelling Christ Principle.

The steward of the feast now appears in our drama. He represents the conscious mind, that attitude in which one is actively aware of his or her thoughts and feelings and has the power to make choices. The steward is the decision-maker. As the steward tasted the wine at the wedding feast, he expressed surprise that the best had been saved until last, for this was not the custom.

How like the steward of the wedding feast we are! We have been brainwashed into believing that at a certain age we begin to fail physically, to be followed inevitably by mental deterioration. The sad fact is that if we believe this, it becomes a part of our reality, even though it need not.

How many of us once believed that after a certain age life would no longer have value? Yet, surprisingly, when that date appears, we feel no different. A lady once told me, "You know I'm just *awfully old!* It seems so strange because I don't feel any different, and I look the same!" She was in her mid-nineties at the time.

Like this *young*, elderly woman, we remain the same persons throughout our lives, able to enjoy life to the fullest, perhaps even more than before. We find that life is an ongoing experience of new discoveries, if we simply allow it to be.

How different do you suppose life would be had we and all others been conditioned since birth to believe we could choose to live as long as we wanted, and do it healthfully and with our mental capabilities intact? Then when we had experienced the fullness of this life, if we so desired, we could choose another, either here on earth or some higher plane of being. We could move gently into it, as simply and naturally as walking through the door of one room into another.

If this became a part of race consciousness, would we not live as long as we wanted, healthfully and with full mental faculties. Then when we chose, we would move from one room to another in God's house of many mansions (John 14:2) – in perfect health and with our full mental capacities intact. Through mass belief, "death" may be necessary for us at this particular time in our human experience. We may die, but we need not get sick, feeble or weak-minded to do it.

Man Of Sorrows?

We can be certain that Jesus enjoyed life and bore no sense of limitation. There was a statement attributed to Lentulus, successor of Pilate as governor of Jerusalem, supposedly giving a detailed description of Jesus. It concluded with the statement: "nobody has ever seen him laugh."

What a sad comment! Yet it makes *me* laugh! The quotation has been proven a forgery, added several centuries after the crucifixion. Unfortunately, however, the concept of the man of sorrows has persisted. We can well imagine the laughter such a notion would have evoked from the wonderfully fun-loving Jesus.

Consider this statement: "Let the children come to me, and do not hinder them, for to such belongs the kingdom of heaven" (Matthew 19:14). Can you imagine Jesus' holding a little child on his knee without smiling or laughing with it? Surely not. Nor was there anyone who enjoyed an encounter with the pious of his day more than Jesus. He openly matched wits with the self-righteous Pharisees and in response to their efforts to trick him into trapping himself, stated: "Render therefore to Caesar the things that are Caesar's, and to God the things that are God's" (Matthew 22:21). Surely, he spoke with a twinkle in his eye.

To get a really true picture of the man, Jesus, consider his disciples: twelve rugged young men, fishermen, a tax collector, political zealots, men of the world who followed him over a period of three years at the risk of their own lives. Can we really believe that during those years they spoke of nothing but God and never told a joke nor laughed together? Of course they did!

And the crowds loved Jesus, and crowds are notoriously fickle. It is almost inconceivable to believe that Jesus could have kept their attention for three minutes, much less three years, without humor and laughter.

Life Is Fun!

We see in the miracle of changing water to wine that Jesus was stating emphatically that life right here on earth should be fun. It should be a wedding feast, the most joyous event in Jewish life! Life was not something to be solemnly endured but, rather, to be lived in joy. Jesus turned water into wine for no other purpose than for the people to enjoy the party and the hosts to be saved embarrassment.

This act did not save a life, nor did it restore life to one who was dead. It did not provide food for the hungry, for surely all in attendance had eaten more than their fill. Nor did it speak to social issues of the day.

It simply allowed the enjoyment of the festivities to continue.

Cana, the village where this miracle took place was located in the province of Galilee. In Greek *Galilee* literally means *a circuit; rolling energy*. Jesus had his mountaintop experiences of prayer and meditation. But it was to Galilee, to the activity and energy of life, that he inevitably returned, to teach and to heal – body, mind and affairs.

"I came that they may have life, and have it abundantly" (John 10:10). This was Jesus' message, and at Cana of Galilee he demonstrated his belief in the ongoing joy of life.

The Message Of This Miracle

The important message for each of us in this drama of the wedding feast is that all of life is to be enjoyed, and even when it appears that joy in life or even life itself is running low, it can be restored.

One would not deny that in life we experience seeming losses: the loss of loved ones through death, separation, or divorce. We face financial, relationship and health challenges. Yet, always there is that within us – the soul (Mary) – that becomes aware of our need even before our conscious mind (the steward) knows a need exists. The soul is always in contact with the eternal Christ Principle within us (Jesus), and our physical faculties (servants) are ready and able to carry out the bidding of the Christ.

Nor does the Christ dwell on some lofty plain. Oh, no! The Christ walks right with us in our own personal Galilee, wherever that may be – and joins in the fun!

The Christ message is life – Abundant life! Recognize that God's will for you personally is for the very best of everything – now and always!

Thoughts For Contemplation And Discussion

1. Within each individual is every character, every place and every event in the Bible. The Bible is the

allegorical story of our lives. Give some examples as to how these *characters, places* and *events* have applied to you personally or through some event you have experienced.
2. Jesus performed miracles as "acted out parables" for the purpose of clarifying his teachings. In the story of the wedding feast, what does the changing of water to wine mean to you personally?
3. By practicing daily prayer and meditation, we remain in constant contact with the *Christ of our being*. What does this mean to you personally?
4. Do you believe that all of life can be as joyous as a *Jewish wedding feast?* How can we help make it so?

Inspired Thoughts On The Joyous Life

1. "These things I have spoken to you, that my joy may be in you, and that your joy may be full" – Jesus (John 15:11).
2. "Thou does show me the path of life, in thy presence there is fullness of joy, in thy right hand are pleasures forevermore" (Psalm 15:11).
3. "From a boy, I gloated on existence. Earth to me seemed all sufficient and my sojourn there one trembling opportunity for joy" – Alan Seeger

4. "This also, that I live, I consider a gift of God" – Ovid.
5. "Were the offer made true, I would engage to run again, from beginning to end, the same career of life. All I would ask should be the privilege of an author, to correct, in a second edition, certain errors of the first" – Benjamin Franklin.

Miracles

1. Supply – Water made wine (John 2:8-9).

CHAPTER II

THE FIRST LAW – FAITH

"According to your faith be it done to you"

— Jesus (Matthew 9:29).

At a recent demonstration of a rather unusual healing technique, someone asked if I believed the instruction was worth the time and expense involved in receiving the training. I answered that I believed *faith* was the one healing power. I think I added something to the effect that *what we* place our faith in probably matters very little, whether it be a surgeon's knife or a prune pit buried beneath a rosebush in the full of the moon. *Faith* is the power that does the healing.

Realizing that my answer might sound a bit flip, I added that if the technique produced faith, it was well worth whatever the cost in time or money. I fully believe this is so.

What About Crutches?

A purist might say this is using a crutch. Perhaps it is. But if we need a crutch, is it not better to use one than to fall?

Faith was undoubtedly the most important factor in producing Jesus' miracles. Over and over he commends the individual healed for his or her faith.

To the Canaanite woman of Tyre and Sidon who, was seemingly rebuked by Jesus, but continued her appeal until her daughter was healed, Jesus said, "O woman, great is your faith! Be it done for you as you desire" (Matthew 15:21-28; Mark 7:24-30). To the Roman centurion who asked Jesus to heal his servant, but added, "Lord, I am not worthy to have you come under my roof; but only say the word, and my servant will be healed," Jesus answered the gentile, "Truly, I say to you, not even in Israel have I found such faith... Go; be it done for you as you have believed." And the servant was healed at that moment. (Matthew 8:5-13: Luke 7:6-10). To the leper who returned to thank Jesus for his healing, he said, "Rise and go your way; your faith has made you well" (Luke 17:11-19).

While faith is the one healing power, I believe that Jesus would tell us to use whatever is required to restore or maintain health, as we go about strengthening our faith in God's absolute goodness. Never should we refuse the help of any one of a variety of healing practitioners because of religious beliefs. Until our faith is strong enough to produce the results needed to live a full and joyous life, we should accept help in whatever way we find it.

The poet, Emily Dickinson expressed it beautifully:

Faith is a fine invention
For gentlemen who see;
But microscopes are prudent in an emergency.

It would appear that this was Jesus' philosophy. He did not refuse to heal someone simply because their faith fell short of the ideal and they needed a crutch. If that was their need, he provided the crutch.

For the deaf man with a speaking impediment, Jesus placed his fingers in the unhearing ears and spat and touched the man's tongue and said, "Be opened!" His hearing and speech were restored (Mark 7:31-37; Matthew 16:29-31). For the man born blind, Jesus spat on the ground and made clay of the spittle and anointed his eyes with the clay, then told the man to wash in the pool of Siloam. He did as Jesus said and regained his sight (John 9:6-8). To the man with the withered hand, Jesus said, "Stretch out your hand." He did, and his hand was restored and made whole like the other (Matthew 12:9-14: Mark 3:1-5; Luke 6:6-11). In each of these instances Jesus provided the action that the person in need of healing *believed* was required for them to be healed.

If this were translated into today's terminology, Jesus might have said, "See a psychiatrist," or "Have an adjustment," or "Confess your sins, and be baptized."

Anna

Frank and I worked for many years with a woman in excruciating emotional turmoil. Let us call her *Anna* (not her real name). With her husband, we tried every method we knew to help her, from meditation and prayer to support during her frequent institutionalizations.

One day Anna called and told me she had been attending a church near her home (she had no transportation to get to ours, she guiltily confessed). She really liked the people and they had told her that her problems were the result of her not being a member of their church, not confessing her sins (of which she was convinced she had many), and consequently, failing to receive their unique form of baptism. "Did I think baptism might help?" she asked in desperation.

Indeed, I did, I assured her. This might not achieve a permanent cure, I knew, but perhaps it would bring about the needed peace of mind to begin a healing of her soul.

Suddenly, she had hope, the first glimmerings of faith. She followed through, joined the church, confessed what to her was a multitude of sins and was baptized. She did not yet understand that faith is an inside job. She required action from outside herself. That is where she was in consciousness, and that was all right. It was a beginning.

I heard from her once after that. She was reasonably happy. She was functional. I sincerely believe that Jesus would have approved.

Now, let me assure you that I do not think that a particular church or its method of baptism is a requirement for salvation. It was necessary, however, for Anna and her peace of mind. She needed a crutch and it was better that she have one than to fall. It would have been cruel to show disapproval and launch into a lengthy dissertation of the finer points of metaphysics when she was unable to understand and respond to them. Many years have gone by since I heard from her. I assume she received the needed faith to salvage her sanity, which was really the issue.

Our goal should be to lift our faith to the degree that *crutches* are unnecessary; nevertheless, we should neither suffer nor be less than our best when a crutch we can believe in is available. Life has graciously provided us with many channels through which healing comes. The highest and simplest is the innate realization of our oneness with God and the knowledge that all of God's life, love and resources are constantly poured in and through us.

There are times, however, when we do not achieve this realization or the healing needed. Perhaps we are too subjectively involved. At such times, we should not blame ourselves or refuse help. Like Anna, we should set to work bringing that healing about and seeing it as love in action. Then we should give thanks that help is available and bless those who serve as God's healing channels.

Healing can never be separated from Spirit. We should pray *with* all healing practitioners and give thanks for them, whatever method they use. *All* healing is spiritual, because God is Wholeness.

Faith Is The Power

Regardless of the method used to assist in restoring wholeness to the conditions of our lives, we must always remind ourselves that faith is the power that heals. Faith is the power that prospers. Faith is the power that creates and harmonizes loving and enduring relationships. Faith is the first requisite to making a miracle.

I wish I could take credit for this observation. Obviously, I cannot. Our Bible, both the Old and New Testaments, is full of references to the power of faith. There are so many references in my concordance that I have not even begun to count them. But it was Jesus who really gave *faith* the star billing it deserves!

In the Gospel of Matthew we read of two healings in which Jesus gives total credit to the individual's faith. The first took place while Jesus was conversing with the Temple Ruler, Jairus, who asked Jesus to raise his daughter from the dead (Matthew 9:18-26; Mark 5:21-43: Luke 8:40-56).

As Jesus followed the ruler to his home

> ...a woman who had suffered from a hemorrhage for twelve years came up behind him and touched the fringe of his garment; for she said to herself "If I only touch his garment, I shall be made well." Jesus turned, and seeing her, he said, "Take heart, daughter; your faith has made you well," and instantly the woman was made well.
>
> (MATTHEW 9:20-22; MARK 6:26-34; LUKE 8:43-48)

Note that Jesus did not say, "My faith has made you well" or "Touching my garment made you well." Jesus gave total credit to the woman's faith. He told her, "Your faith has made you well." Jesus recognized and taught the Truth that we cannot successfully look for something outside of ourselves to permanently heal us or bring us good fortune, for that healing, harmonizing, prospering power can *only* be found within.

Immediately after this, Jesus entered Jairus' house, raised the little girl from the dead and told her father, "Do not fear, only believe." (This miracle will be examined in more detail in Chapter V.) He then went on his way, and we read:

> Two blind men followed him, crying aloud, "Have mercy on us, Son of David." When he entered the house, the blind men came to him and Jesus said to them, "Do you believe that I am able to do this?" They said to him, "Yes Lord." Then he touched their eyes, saying, "According to your faith be it done to you." And their eyes were opened.
>
> (MATTHEW 9:27-34)

Again, Jesus asked the men if they believed. He did not say, "Wow, am I great!" or "Just watch me heal." Nor did he say, "According to *my* faith..." He claimed nothing for himself, but proclaimed total credit for the healing to the faith of the men who had been blind.

Prayers And Other Mystical Powers

I would like to share an observation made through my work in our church's prayer ministry that illustrates the importance of the faith of those who request prayer for themselves and others. On several occasions an experience such as this has taken place. Someone greets me at church on Sunday morning, thanks me profusely for praying with them, then reports what can only be described as a miraculous answer to a request for prayer mailed to our ministry.

Naturally, we are delighted at such good reports, though we never take personal credit. The reason for this is obvious. Frequently, it is not until the next day or even later in the week that the letter requesting prayer arrived. Neither I nor any of the members of our prayer ministry had even *known* the need, much less prayed about it specifically.

In no way am I discounting the importance of that letter requesting prayer or in the prayers of thanksgiving offered by our prayer ministry after the fact. I mention these events only to illustrate the mystical power of prayer. In some way that I do not even begin to understand, both prayer and faith operate outside the realm of time and space, as we know it.

Possibilities And Potentialities

I hope by now you are convinced that faith is an imperative for miracle-making. If you need more biblical authority simply look up the word *faith* in your own Bible concordance and read for yourself some of the things Jesus and other inspired persons had to say about It.

But what is faith? we may ask. Is it that mental power which perceives an infinity of possibilities and potentialities, then literally creates that conception out of Its very Self? "Now faith is the substance of things hoped for, the evidence of things not seen" (Hebrews 11:1).

The great Metaphysical Law is that everything begins in mind. There is nothing that exists that was not first an idea or concept in someone's mind. The chair or sofa on which you sit was first a concept in mind before it was formed into an object. The same is true for the car you drive and the house or apartment in which you live.

It is fairly easy to see how these tangible objects first began as concepts in mind. But the Truth is that *all* things begin in the mind, even those we consider intangible.

Poverty begins in the mind. Disease begins in the mind. Loneliness begins in the mind. On the other hand, prosperity begins in the prosperous mind. Health begins in the healthy mind. Love begins in the loving mind. If you are currently facing a challenging situation in which you *really* need a miracle in a hurry, you probably wonder how to change the direction of your faith – especially if you suspect that your beliefs really did have some bearing on the situation.

A very important step in making that change is so simple that it often seems difficult. All you have to do is accept the fact that it can be done, then focus your faith in the direction of that which you want, not on what you do *not* want.

The good news is that if you do not like the appearances of your world, you can change the direction of your faith and change the experiences accordingly.

Whose Desire?

We have examined faith primarily on a theoretical level. Now let us get specific.

For a moment, consider some of the desires you have experienced throughout your life and if you choose to do so, select one in particular and apply these ideas to it. Perhaps this desire is something you have prayed about for a long time. On the other hand, it may be something so wonderful you never dared dream it could be yours.

Where did that desire come from? Did it originate with you? Or is it just possible that this desire was initiated *for* you by God?

Not one of us was created with desires that are unattainable. An idea could not even be conceived in mind if its realization were not at least possible! Consider it for a moment – a desire for which no fulfillment exists... The very concept is ridiculous! It would be cruelty perpetuated by our Creator in its most vicious form. The very fact that you have that desire is *proof in* itself that the possibility of its attainment exists for you personally right here and now.

I hope this challenges your perception of your worth and potential for receiving. It has mine. A belief in unworthiness is a tremendous hindrance to answered prayer and miracle-making. Too many of us have been taught since childhood and have accepted that we are unworthy worms in the dust. The Truth, however, is that we are God's beloved children dwelling in a safe and nurturing universe that longs to pour out all of its blessings to us.

On the other hand, this does not mean that we never misinterpret our aspirations. All of us have made this mistake at one time or another, and this very misunderstanding of what we want is what so often gets us into trouble. We may *think* we want a particular person in our lives, when what we *really* long for is someone who loves us and to whom we can give our love in return. We may *think* we desire specific *things,* when what we *really* long for is the assurance that we are creative, worthwhile human beings. We may *think* we desire money, when what we *really* long for is a consciousness of security and peace of mind.

It is important that we look beyond the symbol of what we *think* we want, to the true desire underlying it. That *person,* those *things,* that *money* is only a symbol. It is imperative that we understand the spiritual reality behind that symbol, to the source of our soul's true longing. Some persons are hesitant in taking this step, lest they be changed into some other-worldly, etheric being before they are ready. This will not happen. To be a human being is holy; you are designed by God to be a human being in the here and now, and your "Father knows what you need before you ask" (Matthew 6:8).

When you seek to know your Spiritual Self through sincere prayer and meditation, an amazing thing happens. Your true desire is not only fulfilled, but you receive the *thing* you thought you wanted or something even better as well. Jesus told us, "...seek first his kingdom and his righteousness and all these things shall be yours as well" (Matthew 6:33).

What more could we ask – fulfillment on the Spiritual level and on the physical level as well.

The Truth is that there is nothing you can desire for which a fulfillment does not exist. If you have a dream, be assured that a fulfillment for that dream exists as part of God's plan for you

If you want success, (and who of us does not?), be assured that your Creator put that desire in your heart because you have something to give to the world that only you can give, something that will bless you and all humankind. If you want companionship (and all of us do), where did that desire come from if not from God? And what of health of body and mind? Can you possibly believe that God desires anything less for you? Can you imagine a god who wants his creation to be sick?

If we accept Jesus as our pattern for successful living, by his own healing examples we must either believe that health is God's will or that Jesus was the greatest charlatan of all time!

Are You Living Or Dead?

Sometimes people come for counseling and confess (almost sheepishly) that they always dreamed of playing a musical instrument or painting a picture or writing a book. Then they add, "But I couldn't do that.

I'm not important. I don't have an education. I'm too old/young/inexperienced/over-experienced..." The excuses are endless.

There is no more important fact of life than this: Only two absolute conditions exist in this three-dimensional plane in which we live and those two are *alive* and *not alive*. You cannot be a little bit alive or a little bit dead, any more than "a little bit pregnant." You are either living or dead (there is no in-between), and you can be sure that if you are reading these words right now, you are alive, creative and living on planet Earth!

If this is so and if you currently experience a desire or aspiration, then it is only logical to assume that the opportunity for fulfilling that desire exists – right here and now!

If you face a health challenge, do not accept it as irreversible, regardless of statistics, age or family tendencies. You are alive and desire good health; thus, the attainment of that desire is possible for you.

If you long to achieve a specific financial goal, never write that dream off, regardless of past or present circumstances. You are alive, and all the substance that has ever existed exists right this minute, as available to you as to the wealthiest person who ever lived.

If you long for friendships or a more intimate, personal relationship, you are neither too old nor too young, too tall nor too short, too dumb nor too smart. There is someone right this minute longing for someone like you, just as much as you long for him or her!

Place no limitations on your dreams. That dream was placed in your heart by God, and God has more good in store for you than you can ever imagine. Set to work right now strengthening your faith that this is so.

Success Saboteurs

Just as we may misinterpret our true desires, we can also be prone to entertaining attitudes conducive to failure. We might think we want something very specific – good health, financial security, career opportunities, friends or family – but on some unconscious level, we persist in sabotaging the achievement of that goal.

Have you ever noticed such a tendency in yourself? Most of us probably have. Early in life we discover that there are certain seductive fringe benefits that go along with being sick or poor or lonely or mistreated.

Shocking? Perhaps so, but who expects a poor sick person to take responsibility for his or her life? What of the individual with no money? No one asks him for help. And the poor lonely soul so abused by others and life in general… Why, she had a constant topic for conversation that guarantees the limelight!

The internal motivators for such sabotage are legion. This is a pretty dark and grim side of the human personality, but if you are not attaining your dreams, if you are not making that miracle you long for, you might begin by making an honest appraisal of some of the fringe benefits that accompany failure and see if any of them apply in your case. Then ask yourself if these are really worth the price being paid.

This self-understanding is an important part of the work Dr. O. Carl Simonton M.D. does in helping cancer patients termed *incurable* to heal themselves. Dr. Simonton's success rate is impressive. Many patients have completely turned their lives around after being diagnosed as terminally ill. If such self-understanding helps to cure a so-called *incurable cancer patient,* or at the very least to improve the quality of his or her life, just imagine the benefits to be derived by applying self-understanding to our ordinary day-to-day challenges.

An Indiscriminate Power

Can you accept the concept that faith is neither positive nor negative in itself, that it simply is? That faith exists as a totally neutral power available to everyone alike? We might compare it to electricity. I have no idea how electricity works, but my lack of understanding in no way prevents my using it. I can turn on a light switch as effectively as the most brilliant electrical engineer!

And electricity is indiscriminate; it is non-judgmental. We can use it to light a room or electrocute ourselves. It makes no difference to electricity. It just goes along, waiting to be used.

The same is true of faith. Faith is such a beautiful word that we tend to associate it with goodness, purity and love, when the fact is that faith can and has been used by Attila the Hun as productively as by Mother Teresa.

A true understanding of the power of faith can be a shocking revelation. It may lead to very intensive and perhaps even frightening self-evaluations, for the spiritual Truth is that every thought, every feeling, every attitude you have ever experienced has manifested in your life in one way or another, to the exact degree that you believed in it or its equivalent.

As previously noted, tangible objects, such as chairs, automobiles and houses begin in mind; seeming intangibles such as disease, health, prosperity, poverty, love and loneliness also begin in mind. Not only these, but *all* experiences of life, even those which seem to *just happen* begin in mind. Contrary to what most of us have been taught, *all* experiences proceed from the *within* to the *without*.

THE FIRST LAW – FAITH

Take an objective look at some of the seemingly difficult situations you have encountered, then consider your past beliefs. If you are totally honest, you probably recognize some correlations.

Such a self-inventory can be startling. And please be aware that this exercise is in no way designed to bring about guilt or suffering. This is not an accusation.

Quite the contrary! Surely, many (if not most) of these events were set in motion long before we were capable of conscious choice and through conditions for which we seemed to have no control at the time. For many of us, however, it is only by coming face-to-face with the seemingly ugliest and most painful aspects of our creative power that we can accept that power as our own and become its master, not its victim.

Surely no one sets out with the intent of making life painful for him/herself or others. We err because of our ignorance of spiritual law. When we understand the totally non-judgmental phase of faith, we see how we have constantly used it in the past, sometimes to our benefit, sometimes to our detriment. Understanding the workings of this law. we are able to forgive ourselves and know it was only ignorance that caused our pain.

The really good news is that even after we have made what may appear to be the world's bitterest blunder, we can change its effects by re-directing the power of our faith *from* the mistake and toward that miracle we desire.

The Power Of Negative Faith

The writer of the Gospel of Mark told a provocative story of the power of what we might term, negative faith. Jesus had just entered Jerusalem for what he knew would probably be the last time.

> On the following day, when they came from Bethany, Jesus was hungry. And seeing in the distance a fig tree, he went to see if he could find anything on it. When he came to it, he found nothing but leaves, for it was not the season for figs. And he said to it, "May no one ever eat fruit from you again." And his disciples heard it...
>
> As they passed by the next morning, they saw the fig tree withered away to its roots. And Peter remembered and said to Jesus, "Master, look! The fig tree which you cursed has withered." And Jesus answered them... "Truly, I say to you, whoever says to this mountain, 'Be taken up and cast into the sea,' and does not doubt in his heart, but believes that what he says will come to pass, it will be done for him. Therefore I tell you, whatever

you ask in prayer, believe that you receive it, and you will."

(MATTHEW 21:18-22; MARK 11:20-26)

This scripture is puzzling in many ways. Why in the world would Jesus curse an innocent fig tree? It seems totally out of character. Numerous attempts have been made to explain it, the most obvious being that if we (like the fig tree) do not produce good fruit (or good works), we wither and die. Undoubtedly, this has merit on a spiritual and human level. Use it or lose it!

However, when considering the importance that Jesus placed in the power of faith, it seems more likely that in this incident, he was illustrating the tremendous power available through faith, *regardless* of its direction. And Jesus' actions in withering the fig tree have been proven accurate by modern science's experiments with plants. Receiving the same essential care, those given loving conversation, beautiful music and prayer thrived. Those ignored, cursed and subjected to loud and raucous music withered and died.

It is important that we realize that we have this same power to bless and to curse, not by placing a *spell on* someone, as in *black magic* or *voodoo*. That would mean we have the power to intrude on *their* free will, and this we cannot do. All too often, however, we unwittingly curse our own dreams. This we can do. Then we wonder why our prayers seem to go unanswered.

If you have a dream, expect to achieve it, expect to make that miracle, regardless of past experiences to the contrary. Accept that dream as God's gift to you. Recognize yourself as capable and worthy of achieving it. Throw away all excuses and fear of failure and with God's help, see yourself moving toward the successful attainment of that dream.

Directing The Power Of Faith

A few years ago Frank and I toured China. A jokester in our group offered this story as the plane took off from Seattle:

"Somewhere over the Pacific Ocean the pilot's voice suddenly beamed over the P.A. system, 'Ladies and gentlemen,' he said, 'I have two bits of news for you. One is good, but the other's not so good. The bad news is we're lost. The good news is that we have a 200-mile-an-hour tail wind. We haven't the slightest idea where we're going, but we're getting there mighty fast!'"

Though such a story is not designed to inspire a passenger's confidence, it does illustrate the power of directed faith. Directed faith, whether positive or negative, acts as a 200-mile-an-hour tail wind, moving us in whatever direction we choose to go.

THE FIRST LAW – FAITH

Knowing that such a power is available, honor your aspirations. Accept them as the notice of a gift to you from the universe, just as you would accept a notice from the postal service of a package's arrival. Be aware of all the good your faith has brought you in the present and past. Your world is a mystical biofeedback machine. Peace, joy, love, prosperity, and health – these might be termed *celestial pats on the back.* They are Spirit's way of letting us know we are turning on that creative power of faith in a constructive way.

What of pain, lack, or loneliness? There is no need for blame. These are only symptoms telling us that our faith needs to be re-directed.

The wonderful news is that each and every one of us has the power to re-direct that ever-present gift of faith. If the direction your life is currently taking does not bring true satisfaction, you can change your mind, knowing that your life will change accordingly. And you have not even begun to imagine the good in store for you!

Realizing that God's will for you personally is the very best of everything, focus on developing a strong, workable faith as the first step in making your miracle. To do this:

1. Use whatever method is available to strengthen your faith, to make you whole and happy. All good is of God. There is no effective method for

bringing good into your life of which God would disapprove. The fruits of your faith nourish your soul and increase your faith daily.

2. Keep a faith journal. Regularly record your successes. Also record any instances where you suspect that *negative* faith may have brought about unwanted results. Frequently, (daily, if possible) read through this journal. It will remind you of how your faith has worked in the past, both positively and negatively, and will strengthen your belief.
3. Convince yourself that it *is* possible to change your negative faith into powerful, positive faith, regardless of seeming past failures. (There are no failures.)
4. Remind yourself regularly that there is no desire of your heart for which a fulfillment does not exist for you, physically as well as Spiritually. To be a human being is to be Divine.

Thoughts For Contemplation Or Group Discussion

1. Faith is the power that heals, harmonizes and prospers. Offer some personal examples from your own life when this has been proven to you.

2. We need not feel guilty about seeking help as we work to increase our faith. All healing is spiritual. On a deep level, how do you feel when seeking help from a physician, chiropractor, psychologist, spiritual counselor, or physical therapist of any kind? What of a dentist or optometrist?
3. "Prayer is not a product of time and space." Can you give a personal example where you have found this to be true?
4. Faith is a gift given equally to all of us. Do you believe this, or does it seem that the gift of faith is not equally divided?
5. Desire is a notice from God that our good is on its way to us. Offer personal illustrations.
6. How may we sabotage our own success? How have you avoided making such mistakes?
7. Is faith really an indiscriminate power? Tell of times when you have used it negatively and positively.

Inspired Thoughts On Faith

1. "According to your faith be it done to you" – Jesus (Matthew 9:29).
2. "Now faith is the assurance of things hoped for, the conviction of things not seen" (Hebrews 11:1).

3. "The dearest child of Faith is Miracle" – Goethe (Faust).
4. "Faith is the subtle chain which binds us to the Infinite; the voice of the deep life within, that will remain...." – Elizabeth Oakes Smith
5. "It is always right that a man should be able to render a reason for the faith that is within him" – Sydney Smith.
6. "Faith and unfaith can ne'er be equal powers; Unfaith in aught is want of faith in all" – Tennyson.

Miracles

1. Healing – Syrophoenician woman's daughter (Matt 16:21-28; Mark 7:24-30)
2. Healing – Roman centurion's servant (Matthew 8:6-13; Luke 7:1-10)
3. Healing – The ten lepers (Luke 17:11-19)
4. Healing – Deaf man with speech impediment (Mark 7:31-37; Mathew 16:29-31)
5. Healing – Man born blind (John 9:1-41)
6. Healing – Man with withered hand (Matthew 1:9-14; Mark 3:1-6; Luke 6:6-11)
7. Overcoming death – Jairus' daughter (Matthew 9:18-26; Mark 6:21-43; Luke 8:40-66)

8. Healing – Woman with twelve-year hemorrhage (Matthew 9:20-22; Mark 6:26-34; Luke 8:43-48)
9. Healing – Two blind men (Matthew 9:27-34)

CHAPTER III

THE SECOND LAW – COMMITMENT

"Commit your way unto the Lord; trust in Him and He will act"

– Psalm 37:6

Perhaps the most difficult part of miracle-making is taking that giant step of commitment. Surely there are millions of unpainted pictures, unwritten books, unpatented inventions half completed or simply waiting in someone's mind for the commitment that brings them into being.

Nothing is ever accomplished without commitment, without either consciously or unconsciously setting goals and moving in their direction. Jesus knew this and was a master goal-achiever!

Can we seriously believe that Jesus simply appeared one day preaching his message of man's divinity without prior planning? Surely not. From reading the Gospel accounts of his life, we find every evidence that Jesus set very specific goals from childhood.

In Luke's gospel we read that when Jesus was twelve years old he went with his family to Jerusalem for the Feast of the Passover. People traveled in groups, and as they began their return to Nazareth, Jesus' parents realized, to their bewilderment, that he was not with the group. We can imagine the alarm Mary and Joseph must have felt on discovering they were a full day's journey out of Jerusalem and their young son was missing.

We know, of course, that Jesus was found in the temple, listening and asking questions of the learned teachers who were, reportedly, amazed at his understanding. His parents seem to have been less favorably impressed. Their initial reaction was to ask why he had treated them in such a way. His much-quoted response, "How is it that you sought me? Did you not know that I must be in my Father's house?" does not seem to have satisfied them entirely (Luke 2:41-52).

It appears that a family understanding was eventually reached, since the story ends with the assurance that Jesus returned with them to Nazareth and was obedient. Nevertheless, this incident clearly indicates that even at the tender age of twelve, Jesus had his goal clearly in mind and was committed to bringing it into being.

Most of our life's dreams are not so precisely in focus at such an early age, but that makes no difference. Part of the good news that Jesus taught and lived is that it is never too late or early to find our dream and follow it.

Dream Vs. Fantasy

A song was popular many years ago and has since become a standard. It begins, "I'm always chasing rainbows, watching clouds drifting by." It continues in this rather mellow mood, then ends with "I'm always chasing rainbows, waiting to find a little bluebird in vain."

Pretty song, but not such a pretty sentiment!

This song was based on the composition by Chopin, "Fantasie Impromptu." A fantasy... My dictionary defines the word as "an illusory image." This is not the end result of a committed goal.

A fantasy occurs spontaneously when we allow our thoughts and feelings to wander with no specific purpose in mind. There are times when this is a good and relaxing thing to do. It is not, however, the action of commitment, for inherent within each commitment is the directed energy and activity that brings our dreams into being.

Some Healings

Jesus entered a synagogue in Capernaum one day and was approached by a man seeking healing for a withered hand. Jesus said to the man, "Stretch out your hand." He did as he was told, and the use of his hand was restored (Matthew 12:9-13).

On another occasion Jesus' disciples drew his attention to a man born blind and asked who was responsible for this condition, the man or his parents. Jesus replied that no one was responsible; the condition existed in order that God could be glorified. In other words, its purpose was simply to be corrected. Jesus spat on the ground and made clay of the spittle and anointed the man's eyes and said to him, "Go wash in the pool of Siloam." The man did as Jesus told him and returned with his vision (John 9:1-41).

Another incident is told of a paralyzed man who was unable to attend a meeting with Jesus at a home in Capernaum because of his infirmity. To help him, four of the man's friends removed the roof of the house, then lifted the paralyzed man on a pallet through the roof and lowered him into the room where Jesus was teaching and healing.

Jesus said, "My son, your sins are forgiven." The man who had been paralyzed then picked up his pallet and left the house by his own power, while the amazed crowd exclaimed, "We never saw anything like this!" (Mark 2:1-12; Matthew 9:2-8; Luke 6:17-16).

What would have happened had these individuals refused to make that total commitment? Would the hand have remained withered and the eyes blinded as from birth? Would the man have remained paralyzed had he refused to face the dangers inherent in being lowered through a roof on a shaky little pallet? Fortunately, they followed through on their commitment to the healing they desired.

Clearly, we have the power to sabotage our efforts by consciously or unconsciously refusing to follow through on promptings received from Spirit. We may desire better health, but continue to eat unwisely or refuse to exercise. We may desire greater prosperity and success, but fail to take the necessary steps required to bring our abundance into being. We may long for love and companionship, yet resist taking an objective look at ourselves and making the necessary changes that draw friends and loved ones to us.

In this world, mental and physical activity go hand in hand as a prerequisite of all accomplishment, and we must do our part. Neither good intentions nor amulets will do the job. When tempted to rely on the rabbit's foot, remember how poorly it served the rabbit! Jesus said, "My Father is working still and I am working" (John 6:17). Even though our marvelous creative capacities are always at work in us and for us, we – like Jesus – must cooperate.

An Essential Ingredient

Commitment is not a terribly popular word today. Many people think of it as a shackle, a noose about the neck, perhaps even punishment of some kind. Nevertheless, making a commitment is an essential part of the miracle model. Once that commitment is made, true miracles begin to take place.

In order for us to make a commitment, we must first set goals. We must honor our aspirations and make the decision to follow through on them – to separate that which we want from that which we do not want.

We humans are goal-oriented creatures. This is our nature. Each of us has within our very brain cells an automatic goal-seeking mechanism. We were designed to set and achieve goals, and unless we cooperate with this innate need, life loses much of its zest. The trigger to our eventual demise might well be simple boredom.

On the other hand, as we set and achieve goals, life takes on more meaning and we discover that success follows success. One goal expands to another and we find that we are happiest when cooperating with life through this wonderful creative process.

Life is energy. Life is Spirit. We as human beings are spiritual energy focused in the most profound manner that, so far as we know, has ever been devised. And we have the power to create, just as God creates.

When we who are made in God's creative image and likeness set a goal and make a commitment to move toward that goal, we provide the pattern around which that universal, everywhere-present spiritual substance organizes and congeals, and all the Power in the Universe rushes to assist us in its creation. Our only job is to focus our energy on that pattern and not allow it to scatter in all directions.

We might compare focused energy to a laser beam. The light from a laser can cut through steel walls. The same is true of focused mind energy. Nothing can stand in its way.

On the other hand, diffused or incoherent energy moves off in all directions. We may compare it to a mind that is always chasing rainbows, watching clouds drifting by. It is involved in its own little Fantasie Impromptu.

Commitment Rule Number One:

Lovingly nourish your goal with the creative energy of commitment.

Aspiration, Respiration And Inspiration

Human beings have aspirations: we aspire toward greater heights. This urge is undoubtedly one of the greatest gifts we have been given and one of our most powerful instincts.

The word aspire comes from the Latin, *spirare*, meaning *to breathe, to desire with eagerness, to seek to attain something high or great; to long, to tower, to rise, to soar*.

In the Old Testament book of Genesis, we read that the Lord God breathed into man the breath of life and with that primal breath, man became a living, conscious being. Symbolically, this was the first activity of humankind and it is literally the first activity of each individual life. Our very first act is to take a great big gulp of air, and from that moment until the day we pass from this Earth, we continue to breathe. This is respiration, the metabolic process by which an organism assimilates oxygen and releases carbon dioxide and other waste products.

The spiritual counterpart of this respiration process is inspiration – the awakening or quickening of our creative impulse. We can no more live without inspiration and aspiration than we can live without the air we breathe. Aspiration focuses inspiration toward a tangible desire. It is the activating force through which all growth takes place.

Adam And Eve

In the creation allegory we find Adam and Eve with their every need met. It seems that nothing was required of them but to sit around, eat fruit and give names to the birds and animals (Genesis 2:16-21).

Can you imagine a more boring existence? Yet theologians have dared call their escape from this static condition the fall of man!

Spiritually interpreted we know that Adam and Eve are not two people, a man and a woman, but the masculine and feminine aspects of generic humankind, the feminine or feeling nature and the masculine or thinking nature within each of us. When the thinking and feeling natures are joined together, or in agreement, creation inevitably results. Not surprisingly, it was to Eve, the feeling nature, that the serpent made its first overture.

The same is true for us. It is generally to our feeling nature (that part of us that feels desire and curiosity and aspires to greater expression) that these subtle promptings first appear. The feeling nature inevitably presents her aspirations to the thinking nature, just as Eve offered fruit to her husband, Adam. By eating this fruit, by appropriating into consciousness the power of independent decision-making, humankind relinquished forever its role as God's infant creation and became a co-creator with God, a being so magnificent that God, the Supreme Creator of all, is able to experience and express life through us. This was not a shameful event, as many theologians have taught, but perhaps our finest moment in history!

A + C = G

The three Synoptic Gospels tell a story about a rich young ruler who came to Jesus asking what he must do to have eternal life. Jesus told him to keep the commandments, which the young man had always done. With great perception, Jesus added that there was one thing more: he must sell his possessions and give to the poor, then follow him. We are told that the young ruler left sorrowfully, for he had great possessions (Matthew 19:16-30; Mark 10:17-22; Luke 18:18-30).

It is tempting to miss the point of this story and turn it into a social message, though it is highly doubtful that Jesus had social issues in mind when he talked with this young man. Jesus certainly had nothing against wealth. Many of his closest associates were wealthy.

But Jesus understood the difference in *having* wealth and being *had by* wealth. That the young ruler had great possessions may not be totally accurate. More likely, the possessions, whatever they might have been, *had him*, for his need of them made it impossible to make the commitment that would have enabled him to achieve his dream – eternal life.

Our preconceived views can also be seen as the possessions that prevent our wholehearted seeking of Truth. The young ruler had the aspiration but not the commitment. Who knows what miracles might have transpired had the young ruler been able to make this total commitment.

The combination of aspiration and commitment is a goal, and we cannot have one without the other. We could create an equation such as $A + C = G$, that is: Aspiration plus Commitment equals a Goal. First, there must be a desire to accomplish, to be something more than we have ever been, to aspire. Then a decision must be made to follow through on the necessary steps to attain that desire. A commitment must be made.

Surely all of us have aspirations for which we may not be prepared to make the necessary commitment. I certainly do. I would love to be a really good pianist. That is an aspiration and a worthy one.

Realistically, however, I know that in order to become a good pianist, there are certain requirements, primarily, taking piano lessons and practicing on a regular basis. As of now, I am not prepared to make such a commitment of my time and energy. Becoming a really good pianist is simply not that high on my list of priorities. And this is all right. The real problem would occur if I kidded myself into believing that this was a goal to which I was committed, then failed to follow through on the lessons and practice. Guilt would be the natural consequence. As of now, I prefer placing my fingers on the keyboard of a word processor rather than a piano.

My years of experience in counseling with people tells me that many suffer the pain of guilt simply because they have not carried through in taking the necessary action to bring about a goal to which they believe they have committed themselves but in fact have not. If you have difficulty understanding this sentence, do not be surprised. This is convoluted thinking, and is even more difficult to live with than to understand!

THE SECOND LAW – COMMITMENT

Commitment Rule Number Two:

A goal is not a goal until a true commitment is made.

What You Want Now

To be achieved, a goal must be something that you want now. The key words are *you* and *now*. How many unhappy people do you suppose are involved in some business or profession, not because they chose it or even wanted it, but because someone else wanted it for them or expected it of them? Consider the individual who follows a parent into a particular business or profession because it was expected, or becomes a doctor or lawyer or teacher or minister because some other person decided it would be good for them.

Unfortunately, there are people who carry goals with them into adulthood that they set when they were children. Never would they allow their six or seven-year-old offspring to make life-altering decisions, yet they follow the direction of the immature child they were twenty or thirty or even sixty or seventy years before.

What did you want to do or be when you were a child? Let me assure you I had no desire to enter the ministry. I doubt that there were any female ministers in the little town where I grew up. From the point of view of family and friends at that time, becoming a minister, for me, would have been, not only an impractical goal, but a thoroughly inappropriate and unacceptable one, as well! Nevertheless, I am a minister and cannot imagine doing anything else.

Careers have been mentioned in these illustrations, but the same principle holds true in all endeavors. A number of years ago when Frank and I built our house, I automatically chose green carpeting. In my childhood we always had green carpets. It was never questioned. It was green, like the grass, restful to the eyes, my mother always said. As a result, without conscious thought I automatically chose green rugs and carpets for my new house. Finally, I realized I was tired of green and Frank confessed he had never liked it.

This may seem a silly example, but how many people do you suppose are driving a particular make of car simply because at one time that had been the "in" car? Or are wearing clothes of a particular vintage or style because it was so becoming at some long ago time and everyone had said it looked so great?

But consider a more serious goal or commitment – health for example.

There was a pool in Jerusalem by the Sheep Gate called Bethzatha with five porticos or porches. The blind, the lame, the paralyzed desiring to be healed came to the pool, for it was believed that when the waters stirred, healing would take place. One man who had been ill for thirty-eight years was there.

"Do you want to be healed?" Jesus asked the man. The sick man answered, "Sir, I have no one to put me into the pool when the water bubbles up. While I'm trying to get in, others jump in ahead of me and push me out of the way."

Jesus looked him in the eye and said, "Arise, take up your pallet and walk."

We read that the man did as Jesus admonished and was healed (John 5:1-16).

Note that the man did not answer Jesus' question directly. Jesus asked if he wanted to be healed, yet the man began to enumerate his difficulties – he had no one to help him into the pool and people pushed him aside and jumped in ahead of him.

Does that sound familiar? Probably. The tendency to make excuses when we should make commitments is all-too common. When the man finally made the commitment to being healed, he got up and walked without even entering the pool.

Another incident in Jesus' healing ministry illustrates the need to make commitments to that which we desire.

Jesus was entering Jericho where his entry was accompanied by great fanfare and excitement. A blind beggar named Bartimaeus who sat by the side of the road, asked what was going on.

"Jesus of Nazareth is passing by," someone in the crowd told him. Bartimaeus cried out, "Jesus, son of David, have mercy on me!" Hearing his cry, Jesus stopped and instructed that the blind man be brought to him, then asked, "What do you want me to do for you?" Bartimaeus replied, "Lord, let me receive my sight." Jesus replied, "Receive your sight. Your faith has made you well." Immediately, Bartimaeus was healed of his blindness (Luke 8:35-43; Matthew 20:29-34; Mark 10:46-52).

Again, the only requirement was that the man state in his own words what it was that he was committed to, what it was that he truly wanted. In neither instance did Jesus take action in any way. He touched neither man. He simply demanded that they state what it was that they wanted, and when they did, they were healed. They made their miracle. Have you stated aloud what it is that you truly want? If not, why not try it?

Commitment Rule Number Three:

Set goals that you choose and to which you are truly committed now. We do not know why the man at the pool or the blind man had previously failed to make a commitment. There may be any number of reasons. But in failing to make that commitment, they remained dis-eased.

Achievable Goals

For a goal to be worth your time and commitment, it must be achievable. From a spiritual point of view nothing is impossible; factually, however, some things are improbable, and the most likely reason for this improbability is that the commitment to expend the necessary energy to achieve the goal is simply not there.

For example, it would be highly unrealistic for me to set for myself the goal of becoming Pope of the Roman Catholic Church. Not impossible, perhaps, but certainly unrealistic. If I were totally dedicated to the proposition that I, a non-Catholic, married, American woman should become Pope, then the possibility exists that it could happen through sheer willpower, though clearly, there are certain obvious strikes against my attaining such a goal. Like becoming a really good pianist, this is simply not on my list of high priority items and I would not be prepared to pay the price of such a commitment.

Becoming President of the United States is most likely another unrealistic goal, even though I meet all the requirements for the job. The fact is that I simply do not have a strong enough desire to become president to make the commitment that its achievement would necessitate. This in no way implies that it is not a probability for another woman in the near future. We have many qualified women in this nation who are fully capable of and desire to administrate the executive office of government. I simply am not one of them. And when we set a goal, we must be willing to make the commitment to do our part toward bringing that miracle into being.

What Is Realistic?

The question of what is and is not realistic should not be taken lightly. Again, the healing miracles of Jesus offer illustrations.

Jesus entered Bethsaida where a blind man was brought to him. He took the blind man by the hand, led him away from the village, then spit on the man's eyes and laid his hands on him. Spittle was believed by the people of that day to have curative effects. Jesus then asked the man, "Do you see anything?" The man's reply is touching: "I see men; but they look like trees walking." Again, Jesus laid his hands upon the man's eyes. When he removed them, the man looked intently and as he did, his vision was restored (Mark 8:22-26).

This is a very important miracle in Jesus' ministry for in it we see an example of persistence in commitment. The man was blind, and even Jesus' healing touch did not bring about an immediate and total restoration of sight. Evidently, some of the blindness was removed, but his vision was still blurred. A second treatment by Jesus was required.

After this second touch, the man looked with great concentration; he made every effort to see. And as he did, his miracle took place. He saw clearly.

If you have a goal and have made the commitment to bring it into being and nothing seems to happen, remember the blind man from Bethsaida. Is your dream worth as much to you as sight was to him? It took persistence to make his miracle, even with Jesus at his side. But his reward was the priceless gift of vision.

Commitment Rule Number Four:

After you have set your goal and made the commitment to bring it into being, persist in your efforts. Do not give up prematurely.

Keep It To Yourself!

As you work toward making your goal a reality, it is wise to avoid discussing it except with those who will support you in its achievement or appropriately assist in bringing it about.

Jesus was approached by a man who had leprosy. Undoubtedly, the man had suffered emotionally, as well as physically. Lepers were untouchable and required by law to live away from everyone else. Elaborate rules were laid down in the book of Leviticus regarding the conduct of lepers, and they were not allowed to return to their community until a priest examined them and pronounced them clean (Leviticus 13:45, 46).

The man with leprosy knelt before Jesus, saying, "Lord, if you will, you can make me clean." Jesus touched the man considered by society to be untouchable and said to him, "I will; be clean." Immediately, the man was healed of his condition. Then Jesus told him, "See that you say nothing to any one; but go, show yourself to the priest, and offer the gift that Moses commanded, for a proof to the people" (Matthew 8:1-4). Note that Jesus in no way flaunted the laws of the land.

On another occasion, two blind men followed Jesus, crying to him, "Have mercy on us, son of David." As they approached, Jesus asked if they believed they could be healed. "Yes, Lord," both replied. Then Jesus touched their eyes and said, "According to your faith be it done to you." Their eyes were healed, and Jesus sternly admonished them to tell no one (Matthew 9:17-34).

A ruler of the temple, Jairus, had a little daughter who was at the point of death. He came to Jesus and requested that he come and lay hands on her so that she might be healed. While they were still talking, someone from the ruler's home arrived and informed them that the child had died. Undaunted, Jesus proceeded to the ruler's house and raised the child from the dead, then strictly charged the parents that no one should be told what had taken place (Matthew 9:18-26; Mark 6:21-43; Luke 8:40-56).

Why did Jesus tell these persons not to discuss their healings, while in other instances he told them to spread the word? Perhaps he felt that some were not totally convinced of the permanence of their healing and he wanted to warn them of how easily power can be dissipated through idle words.

If you face a health challenge, you should certainly consult a health care specialist. If you have a personal challenge, a qualified counselor can be of immeasurable help. If you have a prosperity need, a financial advisor or consultant can be of assistance. And in every challenge, your spiritual leader is of inestimable value in counsel and prayer work. By no means should you keep everything to yourself.

But the useless chatter regarding our goals is like planting a seed, then going out and digging it up to see if it has sprouted.

Remember, the seed of your miracle grows in God's silence.

COMMITMENT RULE NUMBER FIVE:

Speak of your dream only with those who will support your endeavor or assist in its fruition. Refrain from idle discussion.

Thoughts For Contemplation Or Group Discussion The Five Commitment Rules

1. We should lovingly nourish our goals with the creative energy of commitment. Share times when you have succeeded in doing this and times when you have failed to do so. What was the result?
2. A goal is not a goal until a commitment is made. Without a commitment it remains a dream or fantasy. Share some instances when a full commitment to a goal was made by you and another when it was not? What was the difference?
3. We must make sure our goals are *our* goals *now*. Have you ever followed through on someone else's goals for yourself? What was the result?

4. Once a goal is decided upon, it is worthwhile (unless we consciously change our minds regarding it). To achieve it, we must persist! Share instances of goals set for which you have changed your mind? If comfortable in doing so, explain why. Tell of instances when a goal was set and carried through to completion.
5. We must refrain from idle discussion about our goals. Are there any instances where you talked your goal out of being? How? Why?

Inspired Thoughts On Commitment

1. Father, into thy hands I commit my spirit!" – Jesus (Luke 23:46).
2. "Commit your way unto the Lord; Trust in Him, and He will act" (Psalms 37:5).
3. "Attempt the end and never stand to doubt; Nothing's so hard, but search will find it out" – Herrick.
4. "Water continually dropping will wear hard rocks hollow" – Plutarch.
5. "For what I will, I will, and there an end" – Shakespeare. (Two Gentlemen of Verona.).

Miracles

1. Healing – Man with the withered hand (Matthew 12:9-14; Mark 3:1-6; Luke 6:6-11)
2. Healing – Man born blind (John 9:1-41)
3. Healing – Paralytic (Mark 2:1-12; Matthew 9:2-8; Luke 6:17-26)
4. Healing – Lame man by the pool for thirty-eight years (Luke 14:1-6)
5. Healing – Blind beggar at Jericho (Luke 18:36-43; Matthew 20:29-34; Luke 6:12-14)
6. Healing – Blind man, who "saw men…like trees walking" (Mark 8:22-26)
7. Healing – A leper (Matthew 8:2-4; Mark 1:40-46; Luke 6:12-14)
8. Healing – Two blind men (Matthew 9:27-34)
9. Overcoming death – Jairus' daughter (Matthew 9:18-26; Mark 6:21-43; Luke 8:40-56)

CHAPTER IV

THE THIRD LAW – RELAXATION

"Come away by yourselves to a lonely place, and rest a while"

– Jesus (Mark 6:31).

A story is told about Robert Ingersoll, orator, politician and self-proclaimed agnostic. While visiting theologian, Henry Ward Beecher, he noted an unusual globe of the constellations and stars.

After close examination, he stated excitedly, "This is just what I've been looking for." Then he asked, "Who made it?"

"Who made it?" Beecher chided in mock astonishment, "Why, Colonel Ingersoll, nobody made it; it just happened!"

Like Henry Ward Beecher, every true seeker knows that nothing *just happens.* Everything requires preparation.

Preparation For New Ideas

If preparation is necessary to make a globe or create a universe, how much more necessary it is for the achievement of our goals! Our minds must be prepared to accept new ideas in much the same way that the soil in a field must be prepared before planting the seeds that eventually become a garden.

An important factor in this mental preparation is that of relaxation. The body is an amenable instrument. Most of the tenseness we experience is the result of tense thoughts and anxious feelings and has little to do with our physical organism. Miracles can and do come into being during times of emotional stress, but relaxation of mind and body makes it so much easier!

Relaxation of mind and body is an inherent part of the creative process. There is nothing mystical or mysterious about this. The subjective mind unquestioningly carries out the conscious mind's orders, and it is much more easily contacted and programmed when the necessity to fight through myriad strains and stresses is removed.

A relaxation exercise is usually begun with closed eyes, though this is not necessary. Some people prefer to fix their gaze on a particular object. Some can even successfully meditate as they jog or walk. For most of us, however, sitting quietly with closed eyes removes visual distractions.

Each time we begin to relax or meditate, we should consciously clear our minds. This is not always easy. Our thoughts and emotions are sometimes like undisciplined children. They have intruded at will for a lifetime, and many of us have instantly stopped everything to listen to them and follow their bidding. As a result, these thoughts and emotions become ever-increasingly insistent. You may discover that you are even more aware of their demands as you attempt to still your mind.

Take Charge Of Your Thoughts And Feelings!

Nevertheless, if you wish to make your miracle, it is time to take charge of these thoughts and feelings, to become their master rather than allowing them to master you. This cannot be accomplished in a forceful manner. The best way to discipline these intruders is to treat them gently, as you would a small child. Speak to them softly, saying something like, "This is my time alone with God. If you'd like to join us, you're welcome, but you must be still and not interrupt God and me." Then assure them that you will gladly address any issue of importance with them at a later time.

Speaking this way to "yourself" may seem strange and even silly at first, but realize that this aspect of your mind is operating on a very immature and self-centered level. Its need for discipline must be addressed. Such reminders need to be repeated over and over, so long as the interruptions continue.

Each time you practice relaxation of mind and body, it becomes easier and faster to reach the desired state. If this has not been a regular practice for you, remind yourself that your body has become accustomed to controlling you, and it will use every means at its disposal to maintain that control. Your nose may itch. You may feel the need to cough. Some people even experience nausea during this time. I, personally, have experienced all of these and more. This is simply the body's way of maintaining the upper hand. If you persist, however, these annoyances will lessen with each session.

Undivided Attention

The same is true with your thoughts and feelings. Like small children, they are accustomed to having

THE THIRD LAW – RELAXATION

your undivided attention. In beginning attempts at relaxation and quietness, you may be more aware of mental and emotional activity than ever before. With persistence, however, these thoughts and feelings learn that this is a very special, sacred time, and they too become still.

In addition to being gentle, be very patient with these thoughts and feelings. Do not become discouraged by their interruptions, whether they are simple thoughts, such as "What do I want for dinner tonight" or concerns of a more frightening variety. Just remember that these thoughts and feelings are merely attempting to get your attention in the way that has always worked for them. *Habit,* it is called.

After your mind is cleared to some degree, you will probably find it helpful to take a few deep breaths. We frequently add distress to an already tense body by depriving it of adequate oxygen through the shallow breathing that accompanies anxiety and stress. As you breathe deeply, remind yourself that you are appropriating into your entire being all the good gifts that the Universe has for you. As you breathe out, be aware that that which is no longer needed and helpful to you is being eliminated.

Take a few minutes to consciously breathe gently and rhythmically, paying attention only to this breath of life. Lovingly put aside all thoughts and feelings that would interfere. Do this for a short time, becoming very aware of the feel of the peaceful cadence of your breathing before you move on.

Your Bossy Body

Be assured that each time you practice relaxation of mind and body it becomes easier and faster to reach the desired mental state. If this has not been a regular practice for you, remind yourself that your body with its insistent demands has been as accustomed to monopolizing you and having its way as your thoughts and feelings have. The body wants your attention and will use every device at its disposal to maintain that control, as described earlier.

Probably the most commonly experienced meditative disruption is that of falling asleep. Do not be overly concerned if this occurs. Most likely, your life-long custom has been to sleep when your body becomes still and your eyes close. It may even be that you need sleep at this particular time.

Be aware, however, that wonderful and necessary as sleep is, the kind of relaxation which prepares the mind for miracle-making is not synonymous with sleep. If sleep continues even when you are well rested, you can control it by bracing your arm upward on the side of your chair or on a table next to you. If you fail asleep, your arm will drop and this will awaken you. Eventually, the habit or falling asleep will stop. Do not attempt to force yourself to stay awake. *Easy does it* is the rule.

Talk To Your Body

You will doubtless find that most interruptions during periods of relaxation are relatively minor and easily handled. A simple technique to induce relaxation and calmness is to talk to each part of your body, beginning with the top of your head and working your way to the tips of your toes. Tell each part to relax and be still; tell it that you love and appreciate the wonderful work it has done in the past and continues to do so well. You might speak to yourself (silently or aloud) in such a way as this:

> My mind and my body are calm and relaxed. I feel the warm flow of relaxation spreading from the top of my head to the soles of my feet. My head, my scalp, all features of my face now relax. My neck is relaxed and limber. This warm flow of relaxation now spreads over my shoulders and down my back, over my buttocks, into my legs, my feet and all the way to the tips of my

toes, my arms, my hands, my fingers are relaxed and flexible. I take a deep breath and feel this relaxation spreading through my lungs, through my abdominal area and through my pelvic area. All internal and external organs function efficiently and perfectly. My heart beats steadily and rhythmically with God's loving universe. My digestive system is quiet and at peace. I experience perfect circulation, perfect assimilation and perfect elimination in every area of my life – body, mind and emotions. I am relaxed and at peace...

After you have practiced this relaxation exercise, get in touch with the way your body feels, and if there is tension in any part, tighten the muscles in that area, hold them taut for a moment, then, relax. Take a deep breath and breathe directly into that part of your body. Continue to do this, until you feel relaxation taking place.

As you go through your relaxation exercise, you may find it helpful to go back in memory to a time when you felt very good about yourself physically, mentally and emotionally. Re-experience this time as completely as possible, bringing all your physical senses into play. This can be extremely helpful in lifting your spirits if you feel depressed or if you experience a physical challenge. It is also helpful in lifting you to a more creative level.

After Relaxing...

After you spend some time consciously relaxing your body, begin to contemplate your relationship to God and your place in the universe. It is of utmost importance that you take a feeling of absolute trust in God and the Universe into this time of inner communion, for here you create the true sanctuary of your soul.

To assist in achieving this feeling of trust and security, it is often helpful to use an inspirational statement. This is one I find especially helpful: *There is only one Presence and one Power in the universe and my individual world. That Power and Presence is God, and God is Absolute Goodness.*

Or you might prefer to contemplate a familiar statement from the Bible, such as, "*Be still and know that I am God*" (Psalms 46:10), or such reassuring words as these from the twenty-third psalm: "*The Lord is my shepherd, I shall not want*" (Psalms 23:1) or Jesus' statement, "*Peace I leave with you; my peace I give to you*" (John 14:27). The Bible is filled with wonderful, reassuring statements such as these.

As you become more familiar with this type of relaxation technique, you will undoubtedly find inspirational words in other literature and even begin to create affirmations of your own. (We will examine the process of formulating affirmations and denials in more detail in a later chapter.)

The *key* to using these phrases to assist you in relaxing is to contemplate their meaning and repeat the words until they become a real part of you. True, uplifting ideas, such as these, when used repeatedly, replace false, unhappy beliefs that produce pain and suffering.

If thoughts or feelings intrude on this time, do not struggle with them. Just quietly and gently bring the focus of your attention back to this peaceful sanctuary of your soul.

Questions For God

There may be times when you enter meditation with a particular question in mind. If so, ask that question, then, wait in the stillness for the answer to come. Let me share an experience that I had with this type of meditation.

The church where Frank and I served was too small to be comfortable for our increasingly large congregation. Office space was crowded. Youth Education facilities were inadequate. In addition to that, there was *no* parking on Greenville Avenue.

Then one day we found what appeared to be an ideal church building on Walnut Hill Lane. There was a large, comfortable sanctuary, marvelous Youth Education facilities and more than ample parking. We moved in while waiting for our beautiful old building to sell. But sell, it did not. And in addition to that, as we remained in the building on Walnut Hill, certain disadvantages, previously overlooked, became more and more obvious. It was not nearly so attractive as our smaller building (which was totally paid for), and soon it became clear that certain structural problems were arising. An engineer in our congregation warned that if we remained in the building, major repairs would be in store for us very soon. In fact, he said, the roof over the nursery (of all places) was already in danger of collapsing!

Frank and I and the Board of Directors talked the situation over, but came to no conclusion. Moving back to Greenville Avenue presented obvious challenges. Uprooting and moving a congregation is not something to be taken lightly, and it had been only eighteen months since we had moved before. Losing the congregation was an all-too-real possibility. Yet remaining where we were presented significant financial challenges and potential danger.

In The Silence

Though it was a serious decision, both Frank and I were becoming more and more aware of a nagging little voice growing louder and clearer telling us that we should return to our building on Greenville Avenue. However, I was not all too sure that I could trust the voice I heard. Had it not told me the Walnut Hill facility would be perfect?

Or could I have been listening to my *own* voice?

Perhaps Frank and the other Board members felt the same way, I do not know, but the decision was postponed until the next Board meeting.

Frank and I decided to spend a full hour in silent meditation on the Saturday before the Board would meet and decide our church's future. We cleared our minds, yet remained alert to any form our guidance might take.

I do not know what Frank's experience was, but for me nothing seemed to happen for about fifteen minutes. I struggled to make my mind an open channel, but all manner of thoughts and feelings attempted entry. Then suddenly the scripture, "… the place on which you are standing is holy ground" rang clearly through my mind (Exodus 3:5).

This was puzzling. I was confused. Did these words literally mean that the actual ground on Walnut Hill

Lane was the *holy place* for us to remain? A place whose upkeep could drive us to bankruptcy? A nursery whose ceiling could cave in with the first heavy rainfall?

Suddenly, the guidance was perfectly clear to me. The place (in consciousness) on which I stood (the stand I had taken) was *holy.* My message had been received and it was clear.

Frank later told me that he had been guided in the same direction. At the Board meeting the next day, the decision was unanimous that we return to Greenville Ave. Paradoxically, more land and space became available. We purchased an entire building across the street for office space. The rooms we had used as offices made perfect classrooms for our children. Adequate parking became available. The service station across the street was turned into a parking lot. The new owner wanted us to use it. That beautiful sanctuary truly stands on *holy ground.* We could not have asked for a more perfect and love-filled place of worship. When we listen in the silence, God truly answers.

God's Answers

When you use this method of asking a question of God, the answer may or may not come during the time spent in meditation. Do not be discouraged if an answer does not appear immediately. Be assured that it will be there for you at the right time.

Frequently, the answer comes in symbolic form, such as a song that begins to run through your mind, a phrase that appears for no seeming reason (as in my experience) or as dreamlike visual images or other sense perceptions. Perhaps it will appear as an article in the newspaper. If any of these events occur, the key is to determine what that particular symbol means to you – not to someone else, but to *you*.

Most often, during times of meditation we simply experience a quiet sense of knowing that all is well. Neither specific answers nor symbols may appear. It may, in fact, appear that nothing has happened; yet you are left with a strong and tangible feeling of guidance and protection.

There will be times when you enter meditation for the sole purpose of experiencing the love of God. And what higher purpose could this time of communion offer than this?

Most of our interruptions during these periods of relaxation are relatively minor and easily handled. There is even the wonderful possibility that you will sit down to relax and meditate, and achieve a sense of Oneness with God and all of life on that very first attempt!

But there are times when we really need a miracle, and that very need makes relaxation seemingly impossible: if we feel ill, the discomfort of the body may make concentration difficult; if we have a deep concern for our own well being or that of a loved one, the thoughts and feelings that people our minds may make quietness seem an impossibility; when we feel anxiety and are not even sure from where its terrors rise, the interruptions may not seem simple, but constant and laborious.

Persistent practice will remove the normal annoying interventions of bodily, emotional and mental distractions. But how do we handle those intrusions that come from a sick body or a frightened mind?

We have looked at a number of instances when Jesus healed his fellow human beings of physical pain and suffering. We are also told that he healed mental and emotional disorders as well. Among them was a man known as the *Geresene Demoniac* (Mark 6:1-20; Matthew 8:28-34; Luke 8:26-39).

The Geresene Demoniac

As Jesus left the boat in the country of the Geresenes, he and his disciples were met by a man who lived among the tombs. Attempts had been made to restrain this man with chains, but his dis-ease had progressed to such a degree that he wrenched the chains apart and broke them into pieces. Night and day he wandered among the tombs, wailing and bruising himself on the stones.

Even from afar, Jesus sensed the man's torment and spoke directly to the evil spirit: "Come out of the man, you unclean spirit!" he challenged.

The deranged man, in a rare moment of lucidity, rushed to Jesus, fell at his feet and pleaded for help.

"What is your name?" Jesus asked. "My name is *Legion*, for we are many," replied the spirits through the man.

In other words his condition was not limited to one or two mental or emotional disorders. His insanity would have encompassed an entire textbook of abnormal psychology, and the man identified himself totally with each malady.

Then the man from Geresene did a strange thing. He reversed his request and pleaded with Jesus *not* to send this legion of tormentors away.

What a puzzling response! First, he begged to be freed. He then pleaded that they *not* be sent away.

Puzzling? Do we not see this very reaction in ourselves and others at one time or another, though to a lesser degree? How frequently we speak almost lovingly of *my* allergies, *my* depression, *my* pain and sorrow, while another part of us longs to be free of them.

THE THIRD LAW – RELAXATION

It seems that we become so comfortable with our challenges, so accustomed to having them with us that they become a part of our identity and we hesitate to release them, even when the suffering and pain has become almost unbearable. In our confused state of mind, they may even seem a protection, an amulet, against some new and unfamiliar challenge befalling us.

Our unconscious thinking may go something like this; "This is my problem; I've lived with it for a long time. I know how to handle it. But what if something worse befalls me? No, thank you. I'll just keep the problems I have, and not go looking for new ones!"

Jesus did not begin analysis with this man; nor did he delve into the purpose or role this legion of tribulators played in his psyche.

The occurrences immediately following the demon's departure may lend a bit of insight into Jesus' view of the subject. Nearby herdsmen, we read, were terrified when the demoniac was restored to health, and when the people of the city heard what happened and saw the former madman seated, clothed and in his right mind, they begged Jesus to leave the city. It would appear that insanity was less frightening to them than the mystery of healing.

The man who had been healed wanted to follow Jesus, but Jesus told him to return to his friends and tell them how the Lord had shown mercy on him. Note that in this instance, Jesus told him to make known what had taken place. There may be a very logical reason for this.

The area in which this man lived was outside the borders of Palestine in the Gentile territory of Decapolis. In this area superstition, such as belief in demons, was more prevalent than within the bounds of Israel. In urging the man to tell his friends what had happened, Jesus may well have been attempting to offer some enlightenment to all the people, in addition to healing the one.

Anxiety And Other Destructive Emotions

The healing of the Geresene demoniac is a dramatic story, and, fortunately, not a challenge that most of us deal with on a daily basis. Most do, however, live with varying degrees of pressure and stress that can take its toll on our physical and mental well being, not to mention our ability to relax and make miracles.

From the numerous present-day commentaries on the subject, we might assume that anxiety and other such destructive emotions have only recently come into being. Undoubtedly, current pressures and stresses can stimulate anxiety, but it would be unrealistic to believe that such emotions originated with us. Clearly, anxiety was a part of life in Jesus' time, as well.

Consider this incident related in the three Synoptic Gospels: (Mark 4:36-40; Matthew 8:23-27; Luke 8:22-26).

On that day when evening had come, he (Jesus) said to them (the disciples), "Let us go across to the other side," and leaving the crowd, they took him with them in a boat, just as he was. And other boats were with him. And a great storm of wind arose, and the waves beat into the boat, so that the boat was already filling. But he was in the stern, asleep on the cushion; and they woke him and said to him, "Teacher, do you not care if we perish?" and he awoke and rebuked the wind and said to the sea, "Peace! Be still!" And the wind ceased, and there was a great calm. He said to them, "Why are you afraid? Have you no faith?" And they were filled with awe, and said to one another, "Who then is this, that even wind and sea obey him?"

Four Types Of Miracles

As stated earlier, many of Jesus' miracles may be regarded as acted out Truth-teaching. They are object lessons for the purpose of clarifying Jesus' deeper meanings.

Jesus performed four types of miracles: miracles of healing, miracles of supply, miracles of overcoming death and nature miracles. The stilling of the storm is a nature miracle.

It is not difficult to comprehend the character of the nature miracles when we realize that storms occur, not only in the outer world, but also in our inmost selves. Surely, we can all agree that the ability to still these inner storms is infinitely more valuable than the ability to calm storms in the outer world!

The journey across the lake with Jesus and his disciples which ended in the land of the Geresenes began in Capernaum, a city nestled on the northwest shore of the Sea of Galilee. It was the headquarters for Jesus' Galilean ministry. Capernaum is the Latin version of the Hebrew name, Kjar Nahum, which means *Village of Nahum.*

Two meanings of Nahum are *shelter of comfort* and *covering of compassion.* Jesus and his disciples crossed the river to the country of the Geresenes, home of the mad man. This symbolizes moving from a state of consciousness of comfort and compassion (Capernaum) into one in which *lack of control* is the rule, as personified by the Geresene demoniac. During the journey, not surprisingly, a threatening storm occurred, and the disciples became frightened.

Surely, we can relate to this event. In our own experiences there are times when the storms of life seem

THE THIRD LAW – RELAXATION

to threaten our comfortable little boat, our only seeming protection from the negative mire of the world. At such times, we, like the disciples, are afraid.

We need not be. The Christ of our being is always in the stern of our ship, always awake and in the place of control and safe direction for our lives, even when we are filled with fear. The Christ is not asleep. The Christ *never* sleeps. It may seem that the Christ is asleep, but it is *we* who sleep. It is our awareness of the eternal presence of the Christ which falls asleep.

Such aloneness arises because we believe in our own personal powers and discount the need for the Higher Power in our lives. (It is then that the Christ *seems* asleep.) Nevertheless, when our threatened senses remember to call upon the Christ in the stern, they, like Jesus' disciples are able to perceive the awakened Christ presence which, in turn, leads to peace once more.

In this story, Jesus immediately rebuked the wind and said to the sea: "Peace! Be still!" After that, he turned to the disciples and asked, "Why are you afraid? Have you no faith?"

When we experience anxiety, too often we reverse this process. We begin delving into the why's of our situation: *Why* is my heart pounding? *Why* is my skin crawling? *Why* am I so afraid? We add fears to an already troubled situation. We wonder why we have trouble calming down and experiencing that longed-for sense of tranquility.

This was the method of Jesus: First, he denied the *power* of the storm (He rebuked it.) and affirmed, "Peace! Be Still!" Only then did he ask why the disciples were afraid. This might be compared to the handling of a fire in a building. First, the fire fighters arrive to put out the flames. Only after this is accomplished do the inspectors question its cause.

How To Handle Fears And Anxieties

This is the order in which we too should approach the fears and anxieties of our lives. First, we awaken the Christ through prayer and meditation. We then deny the *power* of any negative force in our lives and affirm peace and stillness.

This, however, is not the end of our work, anymore than speaking the word of Truth was the end of Jesus' work. Jesus asked his disciples: "Why are you afraid?"

The first thing to remember as we attempt to still the initial fear is that anxiety is removable, that its effects are symptoms, not causes. We take a giant step toward freedom when we realize this. Never should we allow ourselves to believe that we are hapless victims of tension and anxiety and all we can do is attempt to live with it.

THE THIRD LAW – RELAXATION

Regardless of the intensity of past fears, what other people say, or even the so-called authoritative sources supporting these emotional outbursts, we need not continue to have such experiences. We *can* relax and make our miracles!

The act of recognizing that fear is neither permanent nor a reality is, in itself, an important step in overcoming it. If professional help is needed in achieving this, we should not hesitate to seek it.

When we look face-to-face at the thing we fear, we find it rarely so terrifying as we imagined. Most of our fears are groundless, and those few that do come to pass generally pale in comparison to our imaginings.

When we have faced our fears, we must stand up to them. There is little use in attempting to outrun them, for they are swifter than we. There is a better way, a more productive way. As we stand up to them, recognizing that they have no power but that which we give to them, they almost always dissolve into the nothingness from which they came. Those that do survive have far less power than we have attributed to them!

Perhaps the most helpful way to escalate the power of faith in overcoming fear is to realize what God's will truly is. We may have believed that God's will for us is less than absolute happiness and joy. Perhaps we were taught as children to believe in a vengeful, unloving

God, doling out punishment on those who failed to live up to certain unattainable rules and regulations.

This is not the god of whom Jesus taught. The god Jesus spoke with is an all-loving, all-giving, all-caring Parent to whom he could profess the greatest of all affirmations with absolute confidence, "Thy will be done" (Matthew 6:10).

If you hold to the belief that God's will for you is anything less than perfect health, abundant prosperity and joy in living and loving, then right now is the time to uproot that belief forever. If an anxious thought pops into your mind regarding the possibility of sickness or lack, simply remind yourself that God's will for you is radiant health and an abundance of all-good. If fears of loss of love or loneliness or unhappiness of any kind appear, remind yourself that you are not only made in God's image and likeness and deserve the very best that life has to offer, but God is always with you in a personal, loving, sharing relationship.

Relax, let go and allow yourself, with God's help, to make a miracle! Relaxation is a very important third step in Jesus' miracle model.

THE THIRD LAW – RELAXATION

Thoughts For Contemplation Or Group Discussion

Each day we should:

1. Choose a special time to consciously clear our minds and relax our bodies.
2. Gently discipline all intruding thoughts and feelings.
3. Persist, and be patient with ourselves.
4. Breathe rhythmically and gently, focusing all attention on this *breath of life.*
5. Speak lovingly to each part of our bodies, letting it know that we appreciate its dependable workings. We should tell each part of our bodies to let go and relax.
6. Recall a time and place when we felt very good physically and very good about life in general. Re-experience that event in as much detail as possible.
7. Contemplate our relationship with God until we feel a deep sense of trust and personal love and caring.
(Which of these is most difficult/most easy for you to accomplish? Share your feelings and experiences, if you feel comfortable in doing so.)

Inspired Thoughts About Relaxation:

1. "Come unto me, and I will give you rest" – Jesus (Matthew 11:28).
2. "How calm, how beautiful comes on the still hours, when storms are gone" – Moore.
3. "People are always expecting to get peace in heaven; but you know whatever peace they get there will be ready-made. Whatever making of peace they can be blest for, must be on the earth here" – Ruskin.
4. "The camel at the close of day kneels down upon the sandy plain to have his burden lifted off and rest again" – Anna Temple.
5. "I like work; it fascinates me. I can sit and look at it for hours" – Jerome K. Jerome.

Miracle References:

1. Healing – The Geresene Demoniac (Mark 6:1-20; Matthew 8:28-34; Luke 8:26-39)
2. Nature miracle – Stilling the storm (Matthew 8:23-27; Mark 4:36-41; Luke 8:22-26)

CHAPTER V

THE FOURTH LAW – IMAGINATION

"Then God said. 'Let us make man in our image...' So God created man in his own image, in the image of God he created him..."

(Genesis 1:26,27)

There are two phrases each of us has heard since childhood, which may well be primary causes for many of the problems we face in life. The first phrase is usually spoken in a hopeless sort of manner – "Oh, well, we're only human;" the second with more condescending overtones – "It's just your imagination."

I hope no one reading these words understands the condition of being human as anything less than totally open-ended. There are no built-in limitations. The only limitations for humankind are those we create for ourselves; thus, the phrase, *"We're only human,"* is an erroneous one, with only one purpose: to justify a lack of initiative.

Truly, there is nothing we cannot do or be. We are very literally *human beings* – humans in the process of being. As John's first letter states, "Beloved, we are God's children now; it does not yet appear what we shall be..." (I John 3:2).

Now look at that equally false statement, *"It's just your imagination."* Surely, we have all been told this at least once in our lifetime. Yet, how many ideas, how much creativity, even genius has been stifled by those four words – *It's just your imagination?*

It begins in childhood. The words are spoken by an authority figure with no malicious intent. The purpose is simply to rouse the youngster out of a dream world and back to reality. Nonetheless, it has about the same effect as a soggy dishrag smacked across the face. And that marvelous gift of imagination may never totally recover.

Many people consider the imagination to be a "tool of the devil", a waste of time, something to be avoided by those with *real* ambition and goals. But all *real* achievers know this is not true. Our imagination is the key God gave us to open the door of our Spiritual treasure chest. In early humanity it was the most powerful of faculties.

Twelve Attributes Of Humankind

In an earlier chapter we discussed that from a spiritual point of view, Jesus represented the perfect idea of humankind in the mind of God and each of his twelve disciples symbolize certain aspects of the fully Christed individual. Traditionally, people have referred to Jesus as *the Christ,* and there is nothing wrong with this concept. Jesus so united his human self with his Spiritual Self (the universal Christ *principle)* that there was no place where one began and the other ended.

But he told us that everything he did, we could do also (John 14:12). Become a Christ? Me? You? Surely not!

Yet Jesus indicated that our Creator knows each of us as the *Christ, the Begotten of God.*

Undoubtedly, most of us fall short of this perfection on the human level. This mystical number *twelve* is repeated over and over in the Bible. Spiritually or metaphysically, the number twelve depicts spiritual fulfillment or completion, the fully Christed individual – that which Jesus was, that which we seek to *be.*

Hundreds of years before Jesus and his disciples were born, twelve other men lived on this earth. They were the sons of the Old Testament patriarch, Jacob, and they became the fathers of the twelve tribes of Israel. Note that important number *twelve* again. These twelve sons symbolize the faculties we find symbolized by Jesus' 12 disciples, but at an earlier or more rudimentary level of their evolvement.

Joseph And His Colorful Coat (Genesis 37-50)

Joseph is the son of Jacob that most of us remember from Bible study. He was his father's favorite, the child of his beloved wife, Rachel, and the child of Jacob's old age. Undoubtedly, Joseph was a charmer. He is described as *handsome and good-looking* (Gen. 39:6). He was quick-witted and bright.

The name *Joseph* is from the Hebrew. It literally means *whom Jehovah will add to; Jehovah shall increase; he shall increase progressively.* These qualities could equally apply to the human imagination, for it too is charming, quick-witted and bright.

If we look at the story of Joseph as a metaphor for the imagination, we gain a new perspective as to its value in our lives.

Joseph's father, Jacob, gave him a long robe with sleeves, aptly referred to in the King James Version of the Old Testament as *a coat of many colors.* We can easily imagine this coat of brilliant hue, for the imagination truly clothes the mind in radiance.

But Joseph was also something of a brat. He tattled and lorded it over his brothers. He was a dreamer, and he had a series of dreams that did not set well with his brothers or his father. In the first, he and his brothers were binding sheaves in the field. Joseph's sheaf stood upright and the sheaves belonging to his brothers gathered round, bowing down to him. In the final dream the sun, the moon and eleven stars bowed before him.

Now it was not necessary that his eleven brothers have a degree in advanced psychology to interpret these dreams. They understood, and were not pleased. It was perfectly clear that something had to be done about Brother Joseph, and quickly!

So a meeting of the Canaanite City Council was hastily called. Joseph was placed in a nearby pit to assure his availability, while the brothers sat down to lunch. As they ate and contemplated the situation, a caravan of Ishmaelites on their way to Egypt passed by. The brothers discussed the situation, then decided that the best way to handle Mr. Smart Aleck Joseph was to sell him to their visitors as a prospective slave in Egypt, which they did.

But there is one thing you can always count on when dealing with an imaginative person like Joseph, or with your own imagination. You can be sure that a way out of any difficulty will be found. And in this instance, Joseph did not let us down.

In Egypt, he went from slavery to a position second only to the Pharaoh in power. As a result, he eventually saved not only his father and brothers, but the future Hebrew nation as well.

Most of us are a little like Joseph. He had an excellent imagination, but he had not yet learned to harness it very well. He had not reached Christ consciousness. From Joseph's story we learn that so long as we still make mistakes, we must learn to control our remarkable power of imagination.

The Dishonest Steward (Luke 16:1-13)

Imagination was the primary tool that Joseph so successfully used, and it was likely the primary gift of another gentleman who used it well. Jesus told a story about a dishonest steward caught stealing from his master. He knew he was about to be fired, so he set to work finding a way out of the mess he was in.

When faced with the possibility of prison, rather than sitting back and bemoaning his fate, he got busy and collected as much as possible from his master's debtors, readily discounting a debt rather than losing everything. He was fired by his employer; (Who wants a crooked bookkeeper?) nevertheless, he had made friends with his master's debtors who, as a favor and to show their gratitude, would likely take him in rather than see him reduced to begging or digging in the ditches.

This can be a puzzling parable. Surely Jesus did not commend dishonesty. More likely, he was saying, "Do your best. Use that which is available to meet your needs on your present level. Don't refuse medical help because you believe in spiritual healing. If you're sick, use the resources you have to get well, then when health is restored, medical help will no longer be necessary. And don't refuse a job because you're too artistic. If you're unemployed, get a job. Wait tables or wash dishes. Then when your bills are paid and your stomach's full, you can paint that perfect picture." The dishonest Steward was not very highly developed on the spiritual level, but his imagination was working very well on the human.

Most of us are a little like Joseph and the dishonest steward. Our Christ consciousness is not yet fully developed, but our imagination is going full blast! It would be wonderful if we always focused our imagination wisely. Unfortunately, this is not always the case. All too often we connect our imagination to the exact thing we do not want. Yet even from this we learn.

Getting Rid Of Worry

Have you ever worried? You may not think the act of worrying is spiritual, but it uses a profoundly spiritual law. It uses the imagination. Consider for a moment what takes place when you worry:

A friend once told me of an evening when her husband was late arriving home. She imagined every dire consequence and then some. She visualized the thing she feared most and brought all of her physical senses into the process. She saw herself as a young widow with small children and no means of employment. She heard the words of rejection from prospective employers. She felt the physical pain of an empty stomach, the loneliness, and the grief at the loss of a loved one. It was so real to her that by the time her husband arrived home, his entire funeral had been planned, with even the pall bearers selected.

And all he had done was stop to purchase flowers to celebrate their wedding anniversary!

Most of us can probably relate to this experience to some degree. But we must remind ourselves that it is important to our total health and wellbeing that we not allow these fears and doubts to control our imaginations. The story I just told was not a constructive one for my friend. She lived on the literal level, and was not aware of the power that thoughts and feelings have. The imagination is too powerful to be allowed to run rampant. A number of Jesus' miracles involve the ability to control unillumined imaginings.

An Unattended Funeral

An event is described by the writers of the three Synoptic Gospels that offers insights as to how to protect that miracle you are making from the onslaughts of a negative imagination. It also tells of a funeral that almost, but not quite, took place (Matt. 9:18-26; Mark 6:21-43; Luke 8:40-66).

Then came one of the rulers of the synagogue, Jairus by name; and seeing him (Jesus), he fell at his feet, and besought him, saying, "My little daughter is at the point of death. Come and lay your hands on her so that she may be made well, and live." And he went with him.

As Jesus and Jairus journeyed toward Jairus' home, the healing mentioned earlier took place, that of the woman who had suffered from a hemorrhage for twelve years but whose belief was so great that she was healed at the touch of Jesus' garment. His magnificent statement to her: "... Daughter, your faith has made you well; go in peace, and be healed of your disease" (Mark 5:34) is a masterpiece of a story within a story.

The narrative of Jairus' daughter continues:

> While he (Jesus) was still speaking, there came from the ruler's house some who said, "Your daughter is dead. Why trouble the Teacher any further?" But ignoring what they said, Jesus said to the ruler of the synagogue, "Do not fear, only believe." And he allowed no one to follow him except Peter and James and John, the brother of James. When they came to the house of the ruler of the synagogue, he saw a tumult, and people weeping and wailing loudly. And when he had entered, he said to them, "Why do you make a tumult and weep? The child is not dead but sleeping." And they laughed at him. But he put them all outside, and took the child's father and mother and those who were with him, and went in where the child was. Taking her by the hand he said to her, "Talitha Cumi"; which means, "Little girl, I say to you, arise." And immediately the girl got up and walked (she was twelve years of age), and they were immediately overcome with amazement. And he strictly charged them that no

one should know this, and told them to give her something to eat.

How To Raise Yourself From The Dead

I doubt that in performing this miracle it was Jesus' intent that we enter the funeral parlors of the world and attempt to restore physical life to the corpses of those who have moved on to another experience. At this time in our development, such a power would surely be misused. Jesus' purpose was more likely that of helping us free ourselves from the needless pain and suffering that we bring upon ourselves by the destruction of our hopes and dreams.

In this particular miracle we are shown specific steps we can take to control and direct our imaginations and resurrect our miracle from that which has seemed to be certain death.

Jairus was the ruler of the synagogue, a man of importance in the Jewish community. He came to Jesus asking that he heal his daughter, who was believed to be at the point of death.

Jesus, as always, symbolizes the spiritual I AM, the indwelling Christ of each of us. The synagogue is that place which contains our aggregation of spiritual thoughts and feelings. A constant flow of all kinds of people entered and left a synagogue, just as they do in our modern houses of worship.

How like our own imaginings this description is! A constant stream of thoughts and feelings come and go, in and out of our minds. Some are of a spiritual nature; some are not so spiritual. Jairus, the ruler of the synagogue represents that in us which has dominion over these thoughts and feelings, that part of us which makes conscious choices and is aware when a need exists, then determines the corrections to be made. We might think of Jairus as representing our conscious phase of mind.

Jairus' daughter represents the miracle we want to make, the dream we desire to become a reality in our lives. The little girl is a legitimate, creative yearning that is now mature and ready to manifest, yet is still vulnerable. She was twelve years old. Metaphysically, twelve is the number of spiritual completion.

What miracle do you long for? To gain financial security? To experience greater health and vitality? To fulfill your creative dreams? To know true love and companionship?

Do not be discouraged if this miracle has not manifested in your world. It may be that your dream is still too vulnerable to outer influences to stand on its own.

THE FOURTH LAW – IMAGINATION

Like the little girl, it is still subject to negative slings and arrows that surround it. Unless this dream is carefully protected and nurtured, it may seem to die, just as Jairus' daughter appeared to be dead.

But you have a tremendous power within you to bring this dream into being. That power is your imagination. Most people are not aware of the creative capacity of the imagination. But you are; thus, you can focus that power in directions that bring into being the fulfillment of your dearest dreams. The first step in directing your imagination is to turn to the indwelling Christ, as Jairus did. Jairus asked Jesus to come and lay his hands on the child, that she might live.

Within each of us that part which needs to be lifted from the depths of negativity is raised at the touch of our Spiritual Self, our personal, individual, indwelling Christ. Such knowledge seems inherent in humankind of all ages and places. This very same idea is beautifully illustrated in such children's stories as Sleeping Beauty and Snow White. The princess (soul) seems to be dead, but at the kiss of the prince (the Christ) she is awakened, and we discover she is not dead, but asleep. And a miracle takes place! Life is restored.

This was true for Jairus' daughter and is true for that seemingly dying part of us as well.

Calming Our Thoughts And Feelings

The next step Jesus took in raising Jairus' daughter from the dead was to constructively direct the imagination by stilling the weeping and wailing thoughts and feelings.

A common reaction when we face the seeming loss of a longed-for dream is to give up hope, perhaps to even wallow in our misery. If we expect to revive that dream, we must rise above this tendency and realize that we are not natural; we are supernatural spiritual beings and we must heed Jesus' words: "Do not fear, only believe" (Mark 5:36). The third step in dealing with a fearful imagination and re-directing it is to deny the reality of any power outside of Spirit, and affirm our union with God. This does not mean we should bury our heads in the sand and merrily affirm that all is well when our world seems to be crumbling. Before we can correct a situation, we must be aware that a need exists.

We do not deny facts. Facts exist and must be dealt with on the human level. What we must deny is the reality of a power of negativity, and this we can easily do. There *is no* reality in sickness because there *is no* principle of disease. There *is* a principle of health. There *is no* reality in poverty because there *is no* principle of poverty. There *is* a principle of abundance. There *is no* reality in loneliness or despair because there *is no* principle of despair or loneliness. There *is* a principle of love and life and unity. When we stand firm on principle, all that is not of principle is powerless in our lives.

Professional Mourners

As Jesus and Jairus arrived at Jairus' home, they received word that the girl was dead. But Jesus said no, she was only sleeping. And the crowd laughed.

Our miracle is never dead. It may sleep or lie dormant for a time, but it does not die! Every dream you have ever experienced, regardless of when it took place, is still a part of you – the cowboy you wanted to be as a child, the astronaut, the artist, the writer, or the musician. All of these dreams are still alive and a vital part within you.

But just try to tell this to that aggregation of negative thoughts and feelings, and note their reaction.

But Jesus did just that!

In those days, wealthy people hired professional mourners to attend the dead and the dying. The louder and more intense the weeping, the greater the love and respect for the deceased was believed to have been. (It also added to the family's prestige, for this was an indicator of family wealth.)

In our own lives it is almost as if we, too, have paid professional mourners in our innermost selves. They are the responses we have developed throughout a lifetime. They are on automatic. They wail on cue. Push the right button and they react.

We can imagine the vehemence with which Jesus ejected these mourners from the room where the child was. This was his next step.

If we really wish to make our miracle, we must be equally forceful in removing all tumultuous and confusing imaginings from our consciousness. We must take in only those positive beliefs that generate and sustain the life we wish to build in our consciousness and express in our lives.

After removing the wailers, Jesus took Peter, James and John and the child's parents with him into the room. If we are to support our miracle, if we are to lift it from the tomb of death, we cannot allow anything but the parent thought and feeling that first conceived this miracle to enter our upper room, our place of prayer and meditation. We also take with us faith, judgment and love, so closely associated with the disciples, Peter, James and John.

We too must refrain from listening to the wailers of the world. We must turn off the television or radio commercial that proclaims flu season. We must ignore the faceless authorities known universally as *they* and all the things that *they* have to say about our future health, wealth and welfare. The unenlightened human imagination thrives on all that *they* say.

We must also avoid the so-called friend who would have us remain as we were, for that friend would deny us our miracle. We must protect this young desire, this twelve-year-old child within us, until it is strong enough to stand alone against these wailers.

Speak The Word

The fifth step that Jesus used in this miracle was to speak with authority. He said, "Little girl, arise," and she arose. Words, indeed, have power. When Jesus raised the dead son of a widow, Luke states that "...he (Jesus) said, 'Young man, I say to you, arise.' And the dead man sat up..." (Luke 7:14,15). In the story of the raising of Lazarus as told by John, we read: "...he (Jesus) cried with a loud voice, 'Lazarus, come out.' The dead man came out, his hands and feet bound with bandages, and his face wrapped with a cloth..." (John 11:43,44).

In the book of Genesis we read that all of creation took place through the power of the Word, "And God said..." and creation came into being (Genesis 1).

The same is true in our individual world. The thought and feeling vibrations of the words we speak literally change the shape and form of our world; thus, we can clearly see the importance of speaking only those words that we want to manifest, only words which strengthen our miracle. (In the next chapter we will deal with this law in more depth.)

The sixth step that Jesus used in raising the little girl from the dead was to instruct those who were gathered in the room – the parents and his three disciples – to tell no one. In some instances of healing, such as the Geresene demoniac, Jesus instructed that the person go and tell in order that God be glorified. In the case of Jairus' daughter, he did not. Perhaps there are times when caution must be exercised when speaking of those things dearest to our hearts.

Jesus allowed only those closest to him and the child into the room. Can you imagine the results of allowing the professional wailers to remain? You should speak of your miracle only to those who will strengthen and reinforce your belief in it and yourself.

The last step in constructively directing our imagination was acted out by Jesus when he told the parents to give the little girl food. We too must nourish our miracle through prayer, meditation, affirmation, study, praise, expectation and through surrounding ourselves with positive, loving people and experiences. We must nourish it with joy. We must give it energy and strength through our love. We are told that

Jairus' daughter got up and walked, and the people were overcome with amazement. When we lift our imagination through these steps, even those dreams that seemed dead literally get up and walk! And the negative thoughts and emotions that had peopled our minds are, indeed, amazed.

Utilizing The "Worry" Technique

We need to control our imagination, yet there is much we can learn from it. Just consider what takes place when you worry. Stop for a moment and recall a time when you were *really* worried. Chances are you experienced one or perhaps all of these reactions.

You vividly visualized the thing you were afraid would happen. You mentally placed yourself in the midst of that dread situation. You were aware of the surroundings, probably aware of the people who might be a part of the scene. With an inner ear you heard any sounds appropriate to such a circumstance. You drew on your memory and were aware of aromas, tastes and even the feel of objects that would be a part of this event. You placed yourself right in the middle of this scene and felt to an exaggerated degree all of the awful emotions that would accompany this happening, should it really come into being.

The chances are that the thing you worried about did not come about. (Remember my friend whose husband brought her a bouquet of flowers, rather than widowhood?) Nevertheless, the experience of worry is a good lesson for each of us. Use of the imagination is the same process we use to worry except that you project that which you *do* want instead of mentally projecting that which you *do not* want.

First of all, we have to know what it is that we want. When we worry, we have a very clear picture of what is worrying us. To creatively image, it is essential that we present an equally clear picture to our subjective minds of the miracle we want to produce. The subjective mind does not understand vague concepts and rambling notions, and it is through the subjective mind that we present the pattern we want produced in our world. What the subjective mind does understand and knows how to precisely reproduce is that which is introduced to it through vivid imagery.

Visual Prayer

This is prayer, though you may never have thought of something like worry as being akin to prayer. We might call it visual prayer, and it is one of the most powerful forms of prayer we can evoke.

Most of us were taught to think of prayer as pleading with God or confessing a multitude of sins. This is not prayer at all, but rather, self-pity. Do you like to listen to someone complain all the time? Of course not, and I doubt that God does either!

Prayer has nothing to do with pleading and complaining. Communication with God is raising our consciousness to the level where we know that what we desire is already ours and is God's will for us. Perhaps it is not mere coincidence that so many of Jesus' miracles involved the restoration of vision. The imagination deals with this inner vision.

Use Your Inner Vision

Utilizing the process is simple. Once you have decided on the miracle you want, create a setting within your imagination in which you are experiencing that miracle in its completion in the present moment, in a way that benefits you and every one else.

Try it now as you read. You can pause for a few moments as you follow my words:

Create a clear mental picture of yourself in a situation in which you know that your miracle has already come into being... Choose the setting... Visualize the people who might be a part of this scene... Take note of what they are doing or what they are saying to you... Are there any other sounds of which you are aware? Take a moment and listen... And now note your surroundings... Within your imagination, reach out and touch an object or two. Pay special attention to the way that object feels – the texture, the shape... Are you aware of any particular fragrances that might be a part of this wonderful scene..? Any tastes...? Spend a moment experiencing these physical sensations as fully as you can...

And now think of some of the things you can do with your miracle that will benefit not only you, but all of humankind, even if the connection seems remote..

Now be aware of your positive feelings regarding this event. Within your imagination, your miracle is a reality. Enjoy it! If necessary, borrow positive feelings from past experiences when you felt very good and successful... Totally reject any negative thoughts, feelings or doubts that might pop into your mind. Just feel very positive and expectant about this miracle that is now yours... Be very aware of these good feelings, and allow yourself to feel them as strongly as possible...Now take a deep breath, and feel a real sense of thankfulness to God for this answered prayer.

THE FOURTH LAW – IMAGINATION

A Power-Provoking Exercise

This is a good exercise to help strengthen your ability to direct your imagination in constructive ways. If you are like most people, visualization may be your strongest physical sense, even if your images seem a bit fleeting or fuzzy.

Some people, however, do not clearly visualize. This technique works equally well, regardless of your dominant sense. Use your strongest physical or emotional perception to focus on your miracle in a positive and constructive way, as you continue to develop your other senses. As you do this, you are literally strengthening your prayer life.

Building A Giant Coliseum

When I was a child, like most children I had an extremely vivid imagination. I was frequently amazed when the things I pretended actually came into being. I was aware even then that I was using a universal law that I did not understand, even though I did not hesitate to use it.

We lived in the country. There were no children with whom I could play. As a result it was necessary that I learn to amuse myself. Our home was on several acres, and I would entertain myself for hours by imagining that I was the princess and this was my kingdom. Our house was the palace, the orchard a dense forest. The chickens were my attentive subjects, whom I addressed each day.

Across the road, beyond the cornfield, at just about the spot where the cows grazed, a giant coliseum stood. Now let me make clear that it stood only in my imagination. There were no buildings of any kind, not a barn or even a cow shed. But I saw that coliseum, and there I imaged myself watching magnificent events.

On that spot Texas Stadium once stood, and there the Dallas Cowboys played football. The reality of the outworking of this law really struck me the day I was invited by wealthy friends to share their suite on the fifty yard line! White coated waiters were in constant attendance, just awaiting our call for food and drink. We were treated like royalty. There my long-ago princess observed first hand the creation she so vividly imaged as a child.

I neither take credit for nor disregard my part in the stadium's tangibility. I believe the imagination's ability to create is limitless.

The imagination can restore health to a body or mind that is sick. The imagination can bring prosperity where poverty has been a way of life. The imagination can direct love where loneliness and pain are the rule.

We constantly use our imaginations, conjuring up this and that. Why not use it to bring into being those things that we really want?

This in no way conflicts with Jesus' teachings. He said, "Do you not say, 'There are yet four months then comes the harvest.' I tell you, lift up your eyes and see how the fields are already white for harvest" (John 4:36).

In other words, our human perception sees lack and limitation. We believe that things can only come about in a certain specified way, through a prescribed manner in a particular time frame. Jesus simply tells us to lift up our eyes, raise our vision, lift our inner sight – our insight – and see that what we truly long for – our own miracle – is ours now.

Thoughts For Contemplation Or Discussion Learning To Use Our Imagination In A Constructive Way

We must:

1. Learn to control our imaginations. Stop negative imaging.
2. Recognize that through the imagination we have the ability to make powerful visual prayers. We have always had this ability, and we have always used it – even when we did not realize it or misused it.
3. Image only that which blesses us and all others.

4. Practice positive, creative imaging. We must experience our miracle as fully as possible, as if it were already accomplished in the here and now.
5. Thank God for this answered prayer, its equivalent or something better.
(Consider how you have used these ideas. Discuss the results)

Inspired Words On Imagination

1. "Do you not say, 'There are yet four months, then comes the harvest'? I tell you, lift up your eyes, and see how the fields are already white for harvest" – Jesus (John 4:35).
2. "Imagination is the air of the mind" – Bailey.
3. "There is nothing more fearful than imagination without taste" – Goethe.
4. "When I could not sleep for cold I had fire enough in my brain, and built with roofs of gold my beautiful castles in Spain!" – Lowell.
5. "This is a gift that I have, simple, simple; a foolish extravagant spirit, full of forms, figures, shapes, objects, ideas, apprehensions, motions, revolutions; these are begot in the ventricle of memory, nourished in the womb of 'pia mater,'

and delivered upon the mellowing of occasion" – Shakespeare, ("Love's Labours Lost").
6. "The best in this kind are but shadows; and the worst are not worse, if imagination amend them" – Shakespeare ("Midsummer Night's Dream.")

Miracles Referenced:

1. Overcoming death – Widow of Nain's son (Luke 7:11-17)
2. Overcoming death – Jairus' daughter (Matthew 9:18-26; Mark 5:21-43; Luke 8:40-56)

CHAPTER VI

THE FIFTH LAW – THE POWER OF THE WORD

> "So shall my word be that goes forth from my mouth; it shall not return to me empty, but it shall accomplish that which I purpose, and prosper in the thing for which I sent it"
>
> – (Isaiah 66:10).

An oriental proverb states that "though we cannot keep the birds from flying overhead, we need not let them make a nest in our hair." A great deal of wisdom abounds in these words.

All of us are aware of thoughts and feelings that flit through our minds from time to time. ("I wonder if I'm catching something." "I don't think my boss likes me." "I think he/she's falling out of love with me.") We might even wonder if such thoughts and feelings come from some outside entity.

One of the most important of our responsibilities is to consciously determine which of these thoughts and feelings we will entertain and thus, project into our world through the spoken word, and which of these we choose to discard.

Undoubtedly, the most powerful technique we have for eliminating those albatrosses that periodically hang about our necks is that of *denial*. The word *denial* can be confusing to those who have studied psychology or experienced therapy. Frequently, in counseling and elsewhere we run across people who state (almost proudly), "Oh, I *never* use denials! I don't believe in them. I only use affirmations."

The spiritual technique of *denial* is not to be confused with the psychological act of refusing to face facts, or as sometimes termed, "burying one's head in the sand." Facts exist as a part of human life. Facts must be recognized and dealt with in order to alter our lot in life. We must remember, however, that facts are *always* subject to change, and the place where we begin that change is *within our own minds.*

Remember: we do not deny that facts exist. What we deny is that these facts have power over us and are not changeable.

Exorcising Demons

Jesus said, "Let your words be simply 'yes' or 'no.'" On the occasion when he performed healing by speaking directly to a condition, he was practicing the use of denials, the *no power* of the mind.

One such healing occurred when Jesus was in the city of Capernaum in Galilee. He was teaching on the Sabbath, and the people were astonished for his words were spoken with authority.

In the synagogue, he was confronted by a man who is described as having an unclean spirit (Mark 1:23-26.). This condition (whatever it may have been) caused him to cry out loudly and uncontrollably from time to time. Jesus directly rebuked the spirit, saying, "Be silent and come out of him!"

There may be times when we feel that we have an unclean demon speaking and acting through us. Have you ever asked yourself, "Did I *really* say that? Did I *actually* do that?"

The demon may be an unhealthy way of life; it may be a habit that seemingly controls you; it may be an attitude that causes pain and suffering. Whatever that demon might be, follow Jesus' lead. When the demon rises up, speak with authority, say to it, "Be silent and come out! You have no power over me! You have no reality! God is the Source of my power, and there's no place in my life for the likes of you!!!"

After Jesus spoke to the demon, we read that for a period of time it convulsed the man and shouted loudly through him. Then harmlessly it came out, and the people in the synagogue were amazed at the authority with which Jesus spoke.

To deny the power of negativity that seemingly holds us is not always easy. It sometimes shouts at us. It may convulse our minds and seize our bodies. But if we contact the Christ within, then speak the word of Truth with authority, we are well on our way to becoming the victor.

And Other Infirmities

After this incident, Jesus went to the home of Simon Peter's mother-in-law, who was ill with a fever (Matt. 8:14,16; Mark 1:30,31; Luke 4:38,39). Jesus was beseeched to help her, and again he spoke directly to the condition, in this instance, the fever. When he spoke, the fever left, and she immediately rose and served them.

We have no way of knowing, nor need we know, the cause of the woman's fever. It could have been the result of a physical infection. It could as easily have been the anger of a hot temper or the compulsive passion that sometimes turns to zealousness or the over-intensity of fanaticism.

Regardless of the source of the fever, the principle is the same: we turn to the indwelling Christ of our being and allow it to take charge. We then speak to that fever, telling it that it has no part in us. If we persist, we, like Peter's mother-in-law, then rise and go about our business.

On another occasion when Jesus was teaching in a synagogue, he saw a woman who for eighteen years was bent over and unable to straighten herself (Matt. 9:20-22; Mark 6:26-34; Luke 8:43-48). He said to her, "Woman you are freed from your infirmity," then laid his hands on her, and she stood straight.

Many of us are bent over with varying infirmities. We carry the weight of the world on our backs. Perhaps we feel that family members or friends are unable to function without our supervision. Perhaps we take too seriously the responsibilities of world or local conditions totally out of our control. Perhaps we are fearful of what may happen or *could* happen. Such burdens can actually bend us over and figuratively (and sometimes literally) break our backs. Obviously, this is unnecessary and inappropriate.

In the Bible a woman represents the soul or feeling nature of an individual. Speak directly and with fervor to that feeling that seemingly breaks your back. Determine what it is, and call it by name. Be honest with yourself. Say to that feeling or emotion, "Negativity – whatever your name might be – leave my mind and body! I am now free from all in-firm (not real or solid) beliefs and emotions!"

The Epileptic Boy (Mark 9:14-29: Matt. 17:14-20; Luke 9:37-43)

One of the most insightful of Jesus' healing miracles is told in each of the three Synoptic Gospels. Jesus had taken Peter, James and John with him onto a high mountain, where the transfiguration took place and even Jesus' garments were glistening and intensely white. As they came down from the mountain they found the other disciples and a great crowd arguing among themselves.

Jesus asked what was going on. One man urgently replied: "Teacher," he said, "I brought my son to you, for he has a dumb spirit; and wherever it seizes him, it dashes him down and he foams and grinds his teeth and becomes rigid; and I asked your disciples to cast it out, and they were not able."

Jesus responded, "O faithless generation, how long am I to be with you. How long am I to bear with you. Bring him to me."

They brought the boy to Jesus, and immediately, he convulsed and fell to the ground, railing about and foaming at the mouth.

"How long has he had this?" Jesus asked.

The father replied, "From childhood. And it has often cast him into the fire and into the water to destroy him. But if you can do anything, have pity on us and help us."

Jesus said to him, "If *you* can! All things are possible to him who believes."

The child's father cried: "I believe; help my unbelief!"

Jesus then rebuked the unclean spirit, saying to it, "You dumb and deaf spirit, I command you, come out of him and never enter him again."

The child cried out, convulsed again, then became as a corpse. The people believed him to be dead, but Jesus took him by the hand and lifted him up.

Later, when his disciples asked why they could not heal the boy, Jesus replied, "This kind cannot be driven out by anything but prayer." Other ancient documents add, and fasting.

The Fast

As you recall, this incident began with Jesus, Peter, James and John on the mount of transfiguration. Jesus performed most of his greatest works when in the presence of these three disciples. As we have seen, Jesus' disciples represent the spiritual faculties or powers of the fully Christed individual. Each one of these faculties is vitally important. It would appear, however, that the most significant of these are faith (represented by Peter), judgment (represented by James) and love (represented by John). It was in the presence of these three that Jesus performed his greatest miracles.

When we read in the Bible that someone is on a mountain or a high place, this symbolizes that they are in a high state of spiritual consciousness. The Mount of Transfiguration would probably be as high a state of consciousness as one could hope to attain. Symbolically, we might say that Jesus had just spent time in prayer and deep meditation, and that his faculties of faith, judgment and love were at their peak.

Nevertheless, it was never Jesus' custom to remain in a mountaintop experience of prayer and meditation. Always he came down from the mountain and went into the world to teach and heal – to "be about (his) Father's business."

THE FIFTH LAW – THE POWER OF THE WORD

The same must be true for us. We feel so good and so close to God during times of prayer and meditation that we may strongly resist the need to return to earth and our day-to-day challenges and experiences. If we follow Jesus' example, however, we inevitably come down from the mountain and back to earth again.

When Jesus returned from what was probably his most meaningful meditative experience to that date, did he find peace, loving associates, confidence and cooperation waiting for him? No. He found total confusion.

We can probably identify with this. We have practiced prayer and meditation for a long time. Then it appears we have finally *gotten* it, and we return to our world joyful and filled with lofty expectations and love for all humankind.

Is everything peaceful and serene? Probably not. Instead, we may be met with total disorder: screaming children, a demanding spouse, a neighbor wanting to pursue a longstanding grievance, a co-worker or employer in the midst of one or more crises. It may seem that our inner faculties have revolted and are literally in a state of siege, and we are their victims.

Needless to say, this can be disconcerting. We might take comfort in knowing that it appears that Jesus also had such experiences. He returned from his mountaintop experience only to be met by total chaos – a convulsing child (or young confused spiritual thought) and a group of disciples (supposedly disciplined faculties) in a state of bewilderment. Surely, each of us can relate to his statement, "O faithless generation, how long am I to be with you? How long am I to bear with you?"

Help My Unbelief

But Jesus did not turn away from the challenge, and neither should we. He went to the boy's father, the *parent thought* that conceived this condition, and put the responsibility directly on him. The father immediately began to tell Jesus how bad things were, how endangered his son was because of his condition, then pleaded, "If you can do anything, have pity on us and help us."

Jesus again put the ball back in the father's park. "If *you* can!" he insisted. "All things are possible to him who believes."

Surely, our hearts are touched by the father's plaintive reply, "I believe; help my unbelief!" Have we not felt that way at one time or another?

During those times when we face our most severe challenges (symbolized by the afflicted boy), when our spiritual faculties (disciples) seem to be of no help, perhaps even in conflict with each other and making things worse, these are the very times when it is most necessary to contact the Christ of our being (symbolized by Jesus), take our power of faith, judgment and love (Peter, James and John) and return to the root belief (the father) that conceived this challenge. We must work with this parent belief (Help my unbelief!") until true understanding is achieved and we are freed from the false, seizing condition.

This was apparently one of the more challenging cases with which Jesus dealt. We must remember, however, that it was not difficult for Jesus at all, but for his disciples.

This is true in our lives as well. So long as we work on a challenge strictly on the human level, depending solely on our human faculties, the condition will persist. On the other hand, when, in total faith, we turn it over to our indwelling Christ, a healing begins.

Physicians today would probably diagnose such physical symptoms as the boy exhibited as a grand mal form of seizure disorder, a kind of electrical *storm* within the brain.

We sometimes experience what seems a grand mal problem or *storm* in our lives. It may be a literal illness, such as a seizure disorder or any of the other multitude of *dis-eases* believed by humankind to be incurable; it may be a persistent *reaction* that would enkindle and destroy every attempt at success; it may be a disappointment so deep that we feel we seem to be drowning in the depths of depression and despair.

When these events occur, we should speak the same words to that challenge that Jesus spoke. Say to it, "You dumb and deaf spirit, I command you, come out and never enter again."

This is not intended to appear simplistic. It is not simple. The child and his father had dealt with this condition since the boy's birth. We, too, may have developed negative belief systems right at our parents' knees that affect every activity of our lives. Thus, it is imperative that we persist in our constructive efforts!

When the disciples asked Jesus why they were not able to heal the boy, Jesus' answer was, "This kind cannot be driven out by anything but prayer and fasting."

A fast is generally considered to be the giving up of something. Spiritually, the fast of which Jesus spoke was a strong form of denial – not clinical denial as the psychologist speaks of it, but spiritual denial that insists that this thing, whatever it may be, has no power over us or anyone or anything connected with us. It is nothing attempting to be something! This denial is a strong affirmation of God's constant and enduring love and goodwill for all creation.

THE FIFTH LAW – THE POWER OF THE WORD

Affirmative Prayer

Every thought and feeling that we experience, every word we speak, unless consciously and successfully denied, is a prayer. And *all* prayers are answered. Affirmations and denials may be spoken or unspoken, though the most powerful is probably spoken. It gives life *to* and projects the thought and feeling *into* living, spiritual substance.

The power of the word has been recognized since humankind's infancy. In the book of Genesis, God spoke creation into being (Genesis 1). The Gospel of John begins with "In the beginning was the Word, and the Word was with God... All things were made through him (the Word), and without him was not anything made that was made" (John 1:1-3).

Traditionally Christians have identified this Word as Jesus, the human being who lived in Nazareth. In a sense this is correct; however, the Word must not be limited to Jesus. Jesus was an expression of the Word of God, but this is true for us as well. The Word as used in John's Gospel is the sum total of God's creative power and is immanent in all life.

I recall a sermon I heard as a child based on the following scripture spoken by Jesus: "I tell you on the day of judgment men will render account for every careless word they utter" (Matt 12:36).

That troubled me. I had visions of myself on that fearsome judgment day, quaking before a wrathful, disapproving god, who looked surprisingly like an unsmiling, critical Santa Claus, as I foolishly attempted to explain away my childish babble.

My understanding was immature. There is no such judgment day in the future, nor is there a wrathful, disapproving god. The God taught by Jesus knows only love, and is constantly in the process of bringing harmony into being. And judgment day is taking place every moment of every hour of every day of our lives.

Jesus' statement goes on to say, "For by your words you will be justified, and by your words you will be condemned" (Matt 12:37). Jesus is not speaking of punishment and reward for nice or not-so-nice words, but rather, the law of cause and effect, the natural consequences for our words and actions.

As mentioned earlier in this chapter, we may not be able to keep the birds from flying over our heads, but we can prevent their nesting in our hair, and one of the very important ways to do this is to carefully monitor the words we speak.

Organ Recitals, Etc.

You know the kind of words I mean. The endless organ recitals that follow the innocent question, "How are you?"; the "woe is me!" attitude regarding how bad things are at home and abroad; the contagious economic fear for our nation; our distrust of fellow human beings. It is these miserably unproductive words that must be noted, and exorcised.

There is another side to this coin. This same power of the spoken word also brings miracles into our lives. You have the ability to consciously choose the goals you want to achieve, the happiness you want to experience, then to create affirmations – words that when spoken into that great *Creative Medium* literally shape and form *Universal God-Essence* into the miracle you desire, even more surely than they form depressions and recessions, disease and distrust. This may seem new and strange to you. If this is the case, let me simply say, "Don't knock it till you've tried it!"

As a novice, you may not even know *what* to affirm. This may be true, as well, for long-time students of Spiritual law. A good way to begin is by asking yourself the simple question, "What's bothering me? What is it in my life that needs changing?" You may answer, "Well, I don't feel as well as I'd like," or "I have trouble getting and keeping a job," or "I have trouble getting along with people," or "I just can't make up my mind. I can't make the simplest decision!"

Or you may begin by seriously asking the question, "What is it that I *really* want to achieve?"

The answers you give to your chosen questions are the starting point. These challenges and goals are the things about which you *need* to make affirmations, because affirmations when practiced persistently, can and will change your thinking and consequently, the circumstances of your life.

Even those who have used affirmations for years may have trouble in formulating their own. The truth is that you need not be dependent on any other person's affirmations any more than you would depend on his or her digestive or circulatory system! There are certain rules to follow in constructing affirmations. There are five directives I personally use in making productive affirmations that have been very helpful. Each begins with the letter *P*. Now there is nothing mystical in the letter *P*, but for me, it makes these rules easier to remember. Affirmations must be personal, positive, present tense, picturesque, and persistently practiced.

Personal Affirmations

The first rule is that an affirmation must be personal. That seems fairly obvious. We cannot affirm for another person: only for ourselves. Nevertheless, many of us have set as primary goals, either consciously or unconsciously, the changing of another person. You know the old cliché – "I'm okay. He or she's the one with the problem!"

The fact is we cannot change any other person, regardless of how much we may want to. We cannot affirm another person into or out of a specific relationship. We cannot affirm our spouse into a better job or a more pleasant disposition. We cannot affirm our children into better grades or a different life style. We cannot affirm our boss or coworkers into recognizing our fantastic abilities and potential.

Nor should we want to. If this were possible, then spouses, children, bosses, coworkers and perhaps even total strangers would be affirming all sorts of changes in us!

On the other hand, what we *can* affirm is a change in our *own* attitude. We can affirm that we are worthwhile children of God, deserving of all good. We can affirm that by the simple fact that we exist in this universe, we are worthy of good health, abundant prosperity and loving, caring relationships – of *all* good things!

We can also affirm that the individual with whom we experience challenges is a worthy, deserving child of God. We *cannot* change that person; but we *can* change the way we see him or her. When we do this, a real miracle takes place. The individual either changes or is no longer a part of our lives.

We might put it this way. The subject of your affirmative statement should always be "*I am* the one *I* must change."

Positive Affirmations

The second rule about affirmations is that they must be positive. When we work to effect a change in our lives, we are dealing with the subjective phase of mind, and the subjective mind understands every statement as a positive one. For most of us, the subjective mind deals with pictures and/or feelings stimulated by the words we use.

For example, examine this statement: *I'm on a diet. I can't eat desserts any more!*

What picture comes to mind? Probably the image of cakes and cookies and pies and ice cream, and you feeling totally deprived! You may even be salivating just like Pavlov's dog in response to the simple mental picture conjured up by reading this statement.

And what of this statement: *I don't have a headache.*

What do you experience? Probably something of the way you felt the last time you had a headache, which is certainly not the experience you want to have.

Quickly, now! Affirm: *I feel wonderful from the top of my head to the tips of my toes! I love life and I follow the rules of good diet, exercise and positive, loving thought!*

I recall the experience of a friend. She stated proudly, "I've never had an automobile accident," then experienced one within minutes of her departure. Fortunately, it was not serious. Is it not possible, however, that the picture generated in her mind by that statement may in some way have influenced her reactions behind the wheel of the car?

How then could we reframe these statements into affirmations that do for us what we want?

Instead of saying *I don't eat desserts anymore*, we might affirm, *I choose a healthy, well-balanced diet – one that satisfies my appetite and furnishes me with the nutrition my body needs.* Instead of *I don't have a headache*, we could state: *I am healthy. I feel good. I'm filled with vitality and energy.* Instead of: *I've never had an accident*, we might safely affirm, *I use care and discretion when driving. I send love and blessings to my automobile and to every person on the road!*

Remember also that the subjective mind does not know how to take a joke. It knows only how to take orders, as it sees them. If you laughingly say, *I'm always doing stupid things*, the subjective mind says. *Stupid things! So that's what he wants... I'll get right on it and make him even more successful at doing stupid things!*

The positive affirmation should state explicitly what it is that you really want in terms that your subjective mind can clearly see and understand. An affirmation should state specifically and positively that which you choose to experience, your true intent.

Present Tense Affirmations

The third rule is that an affirmation should be spoken in the present tense. Again, affirmations are tools that change the subjective mind, and the subjective mind does not understand anything about the past or the future. All it understands is this present moment – right now! It is totally literal.

If you say, *I'm going to lose ten pounds so I can wear that gorgeous swim suit I bought last year,* the subjective mind says. *"That's right. You're going to do that."* There the matter rests. The subjective mind is much like a child (and many adults!). It is literal and very good at putting things off.

You may wonder how you can successfully affirm something you know is not factual. Since you know the affirmation is not yet an actuality, is making such a statement not lying to yourself?

The fact is that your subjective mind takes at face value everything placed in it, unless a conscious effort is made to change it. It does this in much the same way that we would delete an error on a word processor or erase a mistake from a blackboard. This is the *denial* or *"wiping out"* process and it is not lying to oneself.

When you state an affirmation that is not a fact at the present moment, what you are doing is forming a pattern for the subjective mind to produce. When making affirmation, such as, *I am now at my ideal weight. I feel good and I look good,* the picture that plays on your subjective mind is of you, looking and feeling your best. The order the subjective phase of mind accepts is to bring that picture into being, and all the Power that has ever existed in the Universe is at your beck and call to make that picture a reality.

Picturesque Affirmations

The fourth rule is to use picturesque words. The reason for this is simple. The words you speak create a visual pattern from which your subjective mind creates.

Do you listen to Garrison Keeler's radio monologue about his hometown of Lake Woebegone, Minnesota? It is all but impossible to listen to his words and not know these people and places intimately. This is because Mr. Keeler uses beautifully picturesque words and phrases. He literally paints a verbal picture for us.

When we make an affirmation, we must do the same. We need to create a verbal picture for our subjective mind to image.

Compare these statements: *I feel good,* and *I feel vibrantly, vitally alive and brimming over with good health and enthusiasm.* Both are positive, personal statements, made in the present tense; but the first statement – *I feel good* – is, at best, unimaginative. It will do no harm, but it will likely not bring about a spectacular amount of change either. This is not the case with the second assertion.

Try this statement: *I have enough money to pay my bills.*

What feeling does this evoke? Relief, perhaps, but it certainly fails to inspire any real excitement. A better affirmation for prosperity might be, *I am a child of God. I have everything I can ever need to live a thrilling, exhilarating and enchanted life. I am rich!!!*

Which statement stimulated the greater visual image and caused the blood to pump through your veins at a more rapid pace? In both cases it was surely the second statement. Remember: the subjective mind is very much like a little child. It thrives on excitement. And this very sense of excitement makes the subjective mind sit up and take note, and, as a result, make that miracle your desire. Remind yourself that when making affirmations, you should use words that trigger long-term emotions and sense perceptions, not at your adult level, but for your inner child, the truly creative one.

Persistently Practiced Affirmations

The fifth rule to follow in making affirmations is that they should be persistently practiced. Jesus told a story, recorded by Luke, referred to as the Parable of the Importunate Widow.

Importunate is an interesting word. As a child I thought it referred to a widow who was a combination of *impertinent* and *unfortunate*. Neither meaning is correct, though she may well have been either – or both. The word *importunate* simply means persistent.

Jesus' story begins:

In a certain city there was a judge who neither feared God nor regarded man; and there was a widow in that city who kept coming to him and saying, "Vindicate me against my adversary." For a while he refused; but afterward he said to himself, "Though I neither fear God nor regard man, yet because this widow bothers me, I will vindicate her, or she will wear me out by her continual coming" (Luke 18:1-8).

A tendency in interpreting this parable is to assume that God is the judge, and we human beings are represented by the widow. We might think that Jesus is saying that the Almighty is sometimes busy or slow in hearing us (perhaps even hard of hearing); thus, we must keep annoying God till we get the attention we seek. Then, after much pleading, the Creator may listen and grant our request, simply to be rid of the constant irritation. The message seems to be that if we pray loudly and constantly enough, God will eventually grant our request just to get us off His celestial back. Right?

Wrong! When we interpret miracles, parables and allegories, *each* character in the story refers to an aspect of ourselves. We need not pester God. God has already given us everything. Our challenge is not to increase God's givingness; the challenge is to expand our own receptivity.

The judge in this story does not represent God, nor does the widow with her persistent nagging symbolize us. The judge represents that part of our creative mind that has not yet understood that we really want to bring about a change in our lives or what we want that change to be.

This inner judge has not yet responded to our pleas because it has probably been hearing such statement as "I'm going to lose weight. Yes, I'll start right after the holidays, or after this difficult project is resolved; or I'll get rid of that habit. That's right. I'll do it just as soon as I'm over this emotional hurdle or, I'll do something about my attitude, and the way I deal with people. Yes, I'll do that just as soon as I can find a group of friends who really understand me!"

Just As Soon As!

Affirmations such as these are unsuccessful because the subjective mind is receiving the directive that something is to be accomplished *just as soon as...* And, like the horse following the carrot on a stick, the subjective mind nods its head and says, "That's right! That's when I'll do it!"

As the judge in the parable is a part of us, so is the widow.

The widow symbolizes that aspect of us which has lost sight of Truth. She typifies a lack of conviction. She desires to make changes. She has been nagging the judge – the subjective mind – for a very long time, but has not been successful in gaining attention because she goes about it the wrong way. But finally, with persistence she gets it right, and because of her persistence she receives that which she desires. That widowed part is then praised by Jesus, if for no other reason than its dogged determination.

Raising Lazarus From The Dead (John 11:1-46)

Probably the most famous of Jesus' miracles illustrates the use of powerful denials and affirmations and uses each of the *P's* mentioned earlier in a fully productive manner.

Lazarus of Bethany, the brother of Mary and Martha, was ill. The sisters sent for Jesus, who told his disciples, "Our friend Lazarus has fallen asleep, but I go to awaken him out of sleep."

His disciples replied something like, "Well, if he's asleep, he'll wake up. What's the rush? He's okay."

Jesus did not deny the facts. He answered the disciples as plainly as possible, "Lazarus is dead," he told them.

Yet they waited an additional two days before beginning their journey. When they arrived in Bethany, a village just outside Jerusalem, they found that Lazarus had been in the tomb for four days.

While Jesus was still outside the village, Martha ran to meet him, saying, "Lord, if you'd been here, my brother would not have died. And even now I know that whatever you ask from God, God will give you."

Jesus replied, "Your brother will rise again."

Martha said, "Oh, yes, I know he'll rise in the resurrection at the last day."

Perhaps Jesus recognized her response as a more politically correct theological cliché of her day than actual spiritual conviction, for he emphatically affirmed, "I am the resurrection and the life; he who believes in me, though he die, yet shall he live, and whoever lives and believes in me shall never die. Do you believe this, Martha?"

"Yes, Lord," she responded. "I believe that you are the Christ, the Son of God." Then Martha called her sister, Mary, telling her that Jesus had asked for her.

Mary rushed to Jesus, fell at his feet and, as Martha before her, cried out, "Lord if you'd been here, my brother would not have died."

Jesus loved Mary, Martha and Lazarus, and he was deeply moved and troubled. He wept.

When they arrived at the cave where Lazarus had been laid, Jesus told them, "Take away the stone."

Martha and Mary were distressed, and Martha pleaded, "Lord, by this time there'll be an odor, for he's been dead four days."

Nevertheless, they did as Jesus told them and removed the stone. Jesus lifted his eyes and prayed, then cried with a loud voice, "Lazarus, come out!" And the dead man came out of the tomb, his hands and feet bound with bandages and his face wrapped with cloth. Jesus told them to unbind him and let him go.

Looking Inward At Lazarus

In studying this miracle, as always let us consider each individual as a part of our own consciousness, rather than concerning ourselves about the outer event or human personality.

Jesus symbolizes *I AM*, the Christ, that eternal spark of divinity within each of us. And what a master affirmer he was! Surely no greater words have ever been spoken than *I am the resurrection and the life; he who believes in me, though he die, yet shall he live, and whoever lives and believes in me shall never die!*

But what does Lazarus represent? Undoubtedly, *it is* something extremely dear to us. It may be a goal. It may be our happiness. It may be the idea of life itself that seems to be waning. But whatever this beloved Lazarus ideal exemplifies, the Truth is that it is not dead, but sleeping, and the understanding *I AM* (Jesus) goes to awaken it.

But Jesus did not go to Bethany immediately on receiving word that Lazarus was ill. He remained where he was for two full days.

The number two generally refers to the spiritual tools of affirmation and denial. The human thing to do when trouble seems to be brewing is to rush right in and DO SOMETHING!

This, Jesus did not do. He remained where he was for two days. We might say that the very first step we too should take in restoring our aspirations or even life itself is to resist rushing off frantically to save the situation. We should remain right where we are and diligently use our affirmations and denials until we understand that there is no power that can destroy our *Lazarus*!

Only after this has been accomplished should we get busy and take action.

Women represent the feeling nature or soul. The soul receives perceptions (intuition, insight, etc.) from its spiritual nature, but it also collects impressions from its human environment, as well (impending illness, danger, opportunities).

The death belief was strong in the case of Lazarus. It was so strong that even the soul (symbolized by his sisters, Mary and Martha), had given up and insisted that he had been dead so long that decay had begun.

There are times in our lives when the death belief is strong in us. It may appear that life has no meaning or purpose; that we have grown old and can no longer enjoy constructive and creative achievements. Perhaps a frightening symptom or diagnosis has loosened our hold on physical life. Perhaps a deeply loved career seems to be coming to an end.

It is this very death belief that brings about sickness and the eventual dissolution of the soul from the body, that which we call physical death. It also brings about the death of our longed-for miracles.

Comfort

There is great reassurance in the story of raising Lazarus from the dead, greater reassurance than even the eternality of life, great as that is! That reassurance is of personal unconditional, everywhere present love.

As soon as Mary and Martha realized that Lazarus was ill they sent for Jesus. For us, individually, this means that even before we are consciously aware that a need exists, our soul (Mary and Martha) is already seeking help from our indwelling Christ, our individual connection with God.

Nor is the Christ of our being merely an impersonal, uncaring principle. This Lord of life loves us in a deeply personal and caring way. Jesus knew there is no death, yet he wept at the sadness of Mary and Martha and the seeming loss of Lazarus.

He did not, however, enter a deep depression. Instead he set to work restoring life. He went to the tomb, that subconscious part where the belief in life had been buried. He gave thanks to God for this demonstration of answered prayer. Then with a loud voice Jesus spoke to that which was seemingly dead: "Lazarus, come out."

In other words, "Conscious Human Life, come out of that tomb where you've allowed yourself to be buried! Get up and get out of there. That's no place for a child of God! Life isn't for burial in a cave, sealed by a stone! Conscious Life Force, get up and get out of there!"

If we feel the vitality or joy of life slipping away, if we experience *burn-out,* we must do the same: Recognize that death can wear a thousand masks, and deny the power of every one of them. There is only life, and life cannot be dead. The joy in life that appears to be waning is only asleep, and the Christ will awaken it, if we allow it to do so.

Then we affirm life: *I am the resurrection and the life! This was true of Jesus, and this is true of me. I believe in life and only life. Life is eternal. Through the indwelling Christ, neither I nor my dreams shall ever die!*

Thoughts For Contemplation Or Group Discussion

1. It is not necessary to deny the facts of a situation. The facts must be recognized to be changed. We deny the power that these acts seem to have over us. We deny any belief that they are not changeable.

2. It is helpful at times to speak directly to the challenges we face, whatever they might be. Forcefully, tell them to depart!
3. We must persist in developing a strong affirmative faith in our indwelling Christ.
4. Watching the words we unconsciously speak is essential to miracle-making. The subjective mind is an obedient servant, with no sense of humor. It takes literally every word that is spoken and unquestioningly goes about the task of bringing that *order* into being.
5. We speak affirmations (affirmative prayer) forcefully and with authority, as Jesus did.
6. Remember the five *P's:* affirmations must be personal, positive, spoken in the present tense, picturesque and persistently practiced.
7. We must remind ourselves that we are loved by life. Our individual soul is always on guard to protect us, even when we are unaware that a need exists. And the Christ of our being loves us, just as Jesus loved Lazarus, and is always there to be called upon and to heal.

(Tell of any experience when you have used any of the above rules to effectively bring good into your life.)

Inspired Thoughts On The Power Of The Word

1. "Let what you say be simply 'yes' or 'no'"- Jesus (Matthew 5:37).
2. "...for by your words you will be justified, and by your words you will be condemned" – Jesus (Matthew 12:37).
3. "It is the spirit that gives life...; the words I have spoken to you are spirit and life" – Jesus (John 6:63).
4. "All words are formative, but not all words are creative. The creative Word lays hold of Spirit substance and power" – Charles Fillmore.
5. "Words, as a Tartar's bow, do shoot back upon the understanding of the wisest, and mightily entangle and pervert the judgment" – Bacon.
6. "Words are the soul's ambassadors, who go abroad upon her errands to and fro" – J. Howell.
7. "Words, however, are things; and the man who accords to his language the license to outrage his soul, is controll'd by the words he disdains to control" – Owen Meredith
8. The word "impossible" is not in my dictionary" – Napoleon I.
9. A word fitly spoken is like apples of gold in a setting of silver" – Proverbs 26:11.

Miracles Referenced

1. Healing – Man with unclean spirit (Mark 1:23-26)
2. Healing – Simon Peter's mother-in-law (Matthew 8:14,15; Mark 1:30, 31)
3. Healing – Crippled Woman (Matthew 9:20-22; Mark 5:25-34; Luke 8:43-48)
4. Healing – Epileptic boy (Mark 9:14-29; Matt. 17:14-20; Luke 9:37-43)
5. Overcoming death – Raising of Lazarus (John 11:1-46)

CHAPTER VII

THE SIXTH LAW – THANKSGIVING

"Father, I thank thee that thou has heard me. I knew that thou hearest me always..."

– Jesus (John 11:41).

Thanksgiving has a long history in our nation. In the autumn of 1621 Governor William Bradford of Plymouth Colony appointed a day for feasting and thanksgiving by the Pilgrims. In 1789 George Washington proclaimed a national day of thanks. In 1863 Abraham Lincoln revived the custom. Since 1941 we have kept the fourth Thursday in November as our Thanksgiving holiday.

What picture comes to mind when you think of thanksgiving? Is it turkey, baked a sumptuous golden brown and stuffed with rich and tasty dressing? Is it pumpkin pie, spicy and tempting? Is it a table surrounded by those you love? Or perhaps the cheering crowds at a football game? These and all other memories are beautiful and meaningful mental treasures when they are the result of our expression of joy in living.

The need to give thanks is much older than our nation and its customs, however. There is a miracle-working power in the praising act of thanksgiving that transcends turkey, Pilgrims, and even football. The need to give thanks is an urge innate in all of us. Undoubtedly, this need is the underlying reason the holiday we celebrate as Thanksgiving came into being in the first place. As Jesus said, "...if these were silent, the very stones would cry out" (Luke 19:40).

By the act of giving thanks, we direct a force used through the ages by those with spiritual wisdom and understanding. When rightly directed, we discover thanksgiving to be the power that corrects inharmony and brings the fulfillment of our heart's desires. True thanksgiving is the final step in miracle-making.

The teachings of Jesus lifted humanity above old race mind concepts of reward and punishment to a new and higher level of consciousness. The following fable illustrates the old way of thinking:

A Fable By Aesop

Once upon a time a hunter took aim with his bow and arrow at a soaring eagle and struck the eagle in the heart, As the beautiful bird fell to the ground he saw that the arrow was winged with his very own feathers. "Ah," cried the dying bird, "how very sharp are the wounds of our own making!"

This story was told twenty-five hundred years ago by a slave named Aesop. Yet, within this tale is a strong moral. We do not hear fables much anymore. They have been replaced by the single metaphor that tells the entire story. The eagle's story could easily be summed up in the word *boomerang*. Many people suffer today needlessly because of a belief in a spiritual boomerang.

The boomerang was originally a curved wooden instrument used by the natives of Australia. When thrown properly, it goes out, curves around and returns to its sender. The Americanized version of the word, "boomerang" has come to mean any act or utterance that backfires on its originator.

Some people, even dedicated students of spiritual law, have the mistaken belief that Jesus taught the *boomerang effect.* During times of pain and suffering, a student may be heard to wail, "Oh, what did I do? What did I say? What did I think to bring this on me?"

Underlying such laments is inevitably the belief that punishment follows error as surely as night follows day. Yet, this was not the teaching of Jesus. His healing of the man born blind clearly shows that in his mind the power of praise and thanksgiving overcomes the boomerang effect: (John 9:1-41).

> As he (Jesus) passed by, he saw a man blind from his birth, and his disciples asked him, "Rabbi, who sinned, this man or his parents, that he was born blind?" Jesus answered, "It was not that this man sinned, nor his parents, but that the works of God might be made manifest in him."

At such a question, Jesus had the perfect opportunity to launch into a lengthy tirade regarding the nature and multiplicity of the man's sins, or at the very least, to offer a *life reading.* He could have presented any manner of reasons for his blindness, ranging all the way from diet to Karmic debt.

But he did not. He stated clearly that the condition existed "...that the works of God might be made manifest..." In other words, the challenge came not to be analyzed, but to be overcome.

We students of Spiritual law might well see ourselves in the story of the man born blind. We can be so cruel – rarely to others, but frequently to ourselves. We are human beings and, though the seed of perfection is planted within each of our souls, there are times when we fall short of that perfection. When this occurs, we face challenges. At such times we must offer ourselves the same compassion we so generously give to others.

Jesus taught this. His ministry differs from the other great religious leaders and teachers of the world primarily in that he stressed the infinite value of *each* individual. He did not speak of punishment. His message was that of a transformation, an evolution in consciousness. And Jesus did more than simply philosophize about it. He went among the people and taught and healed them on the most personal of levels.

Grace

What is this but grace? The concept of grace is so simple that we often have difficulty accepting it. Very simply put, grace is the love and forgiveness of God that changes our consciousness and, thus, removes and frees us from the repercussions of past errors of thought, word or deed. Our part in this process is to gratefully accept this love and forgiveness, and to love and forgive oneself and others in return. When we consider this aspect of God's love, it is easy to understand the miracle-making power in giving thanks for that which is already ours.

The world of Jesus' day did not understand the law of grace. It understood only cause and effect, punishment and reward; justice in its coldest sense.

After Jesus had healed the man born blind, rather than rejoicing with him, the man's neighbors and those who had known him as a beggar began probing to determine his sin. When they finished, the Pharisees entered the scene. They also questioned him at length regarding sin in general and his in particular.

The Pharisees were the religiously educated of Jesus' day. They have been referred to as *lawyers*, but they were not attorneys as we think of attorneys in our judicial system, but as one highly schooled in the laws of theology. We might call them *doctors* of the *religious legal system*. To a Pharisee, regardless of the benevolent works performed, if it did not come through a Pharisee, it was attributed to an evil power.

Within our individual consciousness, there are lingering *Pharisaical aspects*. There may be thoughts that would bind us to outmoded, external forms of religion that offer no understanding or real meaning in today's world.

The man was healed of his life-long blindness by Jesus. This was an act of grace. We, too, are healed by our indwelling Christ. During times of stress, however, these old Pharisaical attitudes may rise up to accuse us and discredit all beliefs that conflict with them. They demand to know – not *how* we were healed, but the *nature* of our sin.

The neighbors and Pharisees were not satisfied with harassing the man born blind. Other Jews joined the Pharisees at his parents' home, where they too interrogated his mother and father. These Jews then returned to the man, continuing their questions and lengthy discourse on sin.

Earlier we mentioned that *Jews* referred to spiritualized thoughts. In the New Testament, however, Jews often represent our established religious thoughts and systems of worship. The Jews were always the hardest to reach with new ideas. They were set in their religion, and most often refused to listen to new teachings.

Like those who came to the man born blind, our intellect rises up in indignation when we seek to rise above old established ways of thinking, when we accept the simple fact of God's love and grace, and when we attempt to free ourselves of the belief in the punishment and reward of a *locked in justice* system.

The restoring of sight to the man born blind is not merely the story of an event that occurred a long time ago in a far away place. All the characters in this story are within you and me. In some areas of our lives, at various times, we are all spiritually blind. As a result, we sin, we make mistakes, for sin is only the failure to live up to our full potential.

But the Christ, symbolized by Jesus, heals our spiritual blindness or ignorance. All too often, however, our neighbors (those thoughts and emotions near and dear to us and those who know our *beggarly* characteristics), along with our inner Pharisees and Jews, regularly return to us and continue badgering us regarding the reasons behind the condition from which we suffered. They ignore the fact that the condition is healed. The focus remains on the problem, not the solution.

All these people – these inner thought people – self-righteously insist that we have sinned, we have fallen short, and we must suffer. (Remember Job of the Old Testament?)

But Jesus affirmed to those divergent and quarrelsome aspects that the blindness had occurred "...that the works of God might be made manifest," that God's love and goodness should express freely in our lives, that we might simply say, "It came to pass. Thank you, God."

Other Healings

Thanksgiving was an important part of Jesus' ministry, and he used each healing as an opportunity to show the power in gratitude to God.

THE SIXTH LAW – THANKSGIVING

Do you recall the story of the Geresene demoniac, the man who lived among the tombs and could not be bound even by chains? He was more greatly feared by the people after his healing than before. They also feared Jesus. We might say they literally "rode him out of town on a rail!" The man wanted to accompany him, but Jesus told him, "Go home to your friends and tell them how much the Lord has done for you and how he has had mercy on you" (Mark 5:1-20; Matt. 8:28-34; Luke 8:26-39).

In other words, "Praise the power of God. Allow that praise to increase your faith and be an example to those who do not yet understand."

Do you recall the woman Jesus met in the synagogue? She had been bent over and unable to straighten her back for eighteen years, when Jesus touched her and she straightened, we read that she gave thanks and praised God (Luke 13:10-21). One cannot help wondering the part that this act of praise and thanksgiving had in her recovery.

The story of the ten lepers (Luke 17:11-19) also illustrates the importance that Jesus placed on the power of thanksgiving.

Jesus was passing between Samaria and Galilee on his way to Jerusalem. As he entered a village, he was met by ten lepers who stood at a distance and cried for him to have mercy on them.

Jesus told them, "Go, show yourselves to the priests."

As we have noted before, lepers were separated from the people until declared *clean* by a priest. The implication here is that this was not an instant healing, but that by the time they reached the priest, the healing was expected to have taken place.

As they went their way, they were healed. But only one of them, a Samaritan, "turned back, praising God with a loud voice; and he fell on his face at Jesus' feet, giving him thanks."

Jesus asked him, "Were not ten cleansed? Where are the nine? Was no one found to return and give praise to God except this foreigner?"

We are not told the fate of the other nine men, but we know that Jesus commended the one who expressed his thanks, saying to him, "Rise and go your way; your faith has made you well."

Jacob And His Tricky Family (Gen. 27-33)

The power of thanksgiving did not originate with Jesus, though in him it was most vividly evident. Nor has its use been limited to the healing of physical ills. Thanksgiving can heal broken relationships as well.

Early in the history of the Hebrew people, we read how the patriarch Jacob demanded a blessing, even though the situation in which he found himself appeared far from conducive to receiving it. As you probably recall, Jacob was the favorite son of his mother, Rebekah. He had earlier tricked his twin, the firstborn Esau, out of his birthright in exchange for bread and a pot of lentils. He then contrived with his mother to trick his aged, blind father, Isaac, into giving him the inheritance belonging to Esau.

Just imagine Esau's reaction! He was ready to kill Jacob!

For health reasons, Jacob and his mother decided a visit to Rebekah's brother in Mesopotamia was long overdue by Jacob.

The law will not be mocked, however. This was a family of tricksters on his maternal side (nor had his paternal grandfather, Abraham, been totally devoid of deceit), and it was not long before Jacob got his! He was tricked into marrying his Uncle Laban's elder daughter, Leah, though he had worked seven years for the younger daughter, Rachel.

Time passed in Mesopotamia, and Jacob prospered. He married his beloved Rachel and became the wealthy patriarch of a large family. Eventually, he decided to return to Canaan, the land promised to Abraham's descendants.

Once again Jacob resorted to subterfuge to possess what he believed to be his, and he separated from his father-in-law with Laban's warning not to return. And so Jacob, his wives, his concubines, their children and servants, along with his herds and other possessions, began the long journey back to Canaan.

As they traveled, a message arrived that struck fear in Jacob's heart. His brother Esau, accompanied by an army, was moving toward them. Frightening thoughts ran through Jacob's mind. Could he ever forget Esau's threat to kill him? Was that still Esau's intent?

But Jacob was a wily fox! Perhaps Esau's blood thirst could be satisfied with gifts or by killing only a portion of the family, perhaps just a daughter, or even Leah…

Here was a situation that could clearly be described as a severe challenge. Jacob had been warned by his father-in-law not to return to Mesopotamia. That avenue was closed, yet he dared not move forward to Canaan. Esau, the original victim of Jacob's deceit, awaited him there with an armed force. As the cliché goes, Jacob seemed between a rock and a hard place!

Three Important Things

Though frightened, Jacob did three very important things: First, he did not resort to trickery, as was his custom; second, he took appropriate action. He sent gifts to Esau, hoping to placate his brother and convince him that he desired that they be friends; and third, he prayed. The entire company moved on while Jacob remained at the ford of Jabbok where "Jacob was left alone; and a man wrestled with him until the breaking of the day." (Gen. 32:24).

Through this event Jacob discovered the power of thanksgiving, he found that out of every experience, no matter how hopeless it might appear, a blessing – a reason for thanksgiving – will emerge if we are able to accept it.

Spiritually, Jacob overcame the fear that had made it impossible for him to give thanks before the blessing manifested. On the human level, he also overcame his severe challenge.

This is a law of nature on all levels. Frank and I saw an example of such an overcoming in the midst of the bleak, hot desert of Jordan. We were in the ancient city of Petra, called the *Rose City* because of the magnificent caves carved from rose-colored rock. We had ridden horses through a narrow cleft which in places was sheer cliff wall rising over a hundred feet straight up on both sides. There seemed nothing but rock. Then we saw it!

In a ridge of rock on our right was a patch of green: a gnarled fig tree. A seed, blown by the wind, had lodged where there was a little soil and perhaps some trapped moisture. It showed its thankfulness for even that little, and clung to the rock, defying its perilous environment and finally overcoming it, expressing itself in paradoxical beauty – life emerging from a rock!

Like the fig tree, Jacob was an overcomer. The man with whom he struggled spiritually represents his higher nature struggling to overcome, to demonstrate to his human nature the force of thanksgiving. In gaining control of *himself,* he made a miracle.

As Jacob's brother Esau and his army of four hundred men approached, we can easily imagine Jacob's fears.

"But Esau ran to meet him, and embraced him, and fell on his neck and kissed him, and they wept (Gen. 33.4). The family feud of years' standing was healed.

It was not necessary for Jacob to experience such trials and indignities. It was not the will of God, but rather the result of erroneous beliefs and acts, the result of Jacob's failure to give thanks for each blessing, no matter how seemingly small, even before they became manifest.

Nevertheless, out of seeming disaster, through Spiritual power, Jacob emerged the victor and went on to become known as *Israel,* the father of the twelve tribes. Esau prospered, as well.

King David And Depression

Another healing to be gained through the act of thanksgiving is the overcoming of mental or emotional depression. King David was a man of many moods, subject to great highs, and to lows equally great. Had he lived today, he might likely have been given thalidomide or other drug and diagnosed as *manic-depressive.*

On the occasion of the fatal illness of his and Bathsheba's infant son, David was so distraught that he fasted and lay upon the ground for seven days and nights. So great was his grief that when the child died, the servants were fearful of informing him (2 Sam. 12.15-23).

(Their reluctance is understandable. At the deaths of King Saul's son and David's friend, Jonathan, the young man who brought David the news was himself put to death. It was not wise to bring bad news to the king! (2 Sam. 1:11,12).

At the death of another son, the rebellious but beloved Absalom, we can readily feel David's suffering as we read:

> ...the king was deeply moved and went up to the chamber over the gate, and wept; and as he went, he said, "O my son Absalom, my son, my son, Absalom! Would I had died instead of you, O Absalom, my son, my son! (1 Sam. 18:33)

Yet, in the overall view of David, we find a man who is happy, wealthy and healthy. He found the secret of the miracle working power of thanksgiving and was able to overcome the periods of depression and return to joy.

When faced with depression, he found great solace in offering prayers of praise and Thanksgiving. (Fortunately for us, many of these are recorded in the Old Testament.) He then took physical action to correct the depressed condition. He played his lyre and sang and often danced. He filled his heart with glad thoughts and manifested that gladness until it became a healing for his mind and body.

King Solomon, the second son of David and Bathsheba, may have expressed a portion of his father's attitude when he wrote, "A cheerful heart is a good medicine, but a downcast spirit dries up the bones" (Prov. 17:22).

Write God A Letter

A technique I have used often and successfully to overcome large and small challenges and to bring many blessings into my life is that of writing a *thank you letter* to God.

I sit down with pen and paper, date the letter in advance and begin, "Dear Father," or Dear Father and Mother." Sometimes I write, "Dear Mom and Dad." I had an excellent relationship with my own parents, so it is easy for me to use the Parental name for God. For one without so good a relationship, any name that evokes a feeling of trust and love is appropriate – perhaps "Dear God" or "Higher Self." The salutation makes no difference. God does not take offense. The thing that matters is the faith generated by this step in gratitude for answered prayer, and that you are writing (praying) to your own personal concept of a loving God.

This is a *thank you* letter, and in it I say "thanks" for everything that I want to take place by the time the date of the letter comes around. Naturally I choose my requests with extreme care. I include such things as health and wellbeing for myself and my loved ones and others who have requested that I pray with them. I also include specific issues with which I am dealing. Nothing is too small or too large to share with my Parent God. Ideally, I write such a letter in advance once each month.

If an urgent need arises, I write at that time also, and give thanks for the outcome I desire. I recall when my little poodle, Pyxie, seemed at the point of death. She was not a young dog and she had already lost so much weight from earlier surgery that she seemed to be disappearing before our very eyes. Our veterinarian was not hopeful. Surgery was required. My faith faltered. Could I possibly ask for her recovery when my own faith was so weak.

But I did, and the next day she was better and the next, even more improved. And within the week she was with us at home. It took a great deal of care and love, but she was as healthy, spry and spoiled as any little dog could possibly be.

No Problems Allowed!

When I write a *thank you letter to* God, I do not write about the problem or why I deserve for it to be solved (this can be a temptation), nor do I ramble or tell God *how* to bring the answer into being. This letter's only purpose is to give thanks in advance for the good I choose to receive. I write the letter several times, making sure that it is worded precisely as I want it to be, then I either fold it and put it away in a Bible or some other special place or let it burn and watch the paper as it turns to ash.

I have experienced miracles as a result of this technique. There have been times (as in Pyxie's case) when it was difficult to write *thank you* for something that my conscious mind did not really expect. At first I had to literally force myself to do so. I can only say that there is much more to us than our conscious mind, and *seeing is believing.*

THE SIXTH LAW – THANKSGIVING

Each of us has much for which to be thankful, but when we feel *down in the dumps* we tend to forget our thankfulness. At such times we might profit from the words of English soldier and statesman, Oliver Cromwell, who prayed, "Some people have food but no appetite. Others have an appetite but no food. I have both. The Lord be praised!"

And the Lord is, indeed, to be praised! Both Jacob and David discovered the power of praise out of necessity. Jesus understood the law by which it operates, and gladly shared it with us. He demonstrated it on numerous occasions, and he also explained it. Jesus did not need a challenge with which to wrestle or depths of despair out of which to climb before invoking the power of thanksgiving. All Jesus needed was a purpose.

When he stood before the multitude with only two fish and five loaves of bread, he lifted his eyes and blessed the food (Matt. 14:13-23: Mark 6:30-46: Luke 9:10-17: John 6:1-16). He gave thanks, and we are told that all were fed, with food left over.

Jesus recognized no limitation, he was a bit like the little boy who listened in rapt attention as the new minister finished his sermon and prayed on in lengthy detail, enumerating the multitudinous needs of humankind. On the way home, the father asked the boy if he had been impressed by so eloquent a prayer.

"I sure was. Daddy!" the son replied. "Why, that preacher asked God for things that other preachers don't even know He has". And so did Jesus.

He even had the audacity to ask God to raise the dead.

Raising Lazarus (John 11:1-46)

Again we return to the story of Jesus' friend Lazarus – dead and buried four days. Jesus stood at the tomb and asked that he be restored to life. We read in the Gospel of John that he first lifted his eyes – he raised his vision from the world of appearances to that of Truth.

He then spoke these words, "Father, I thank thee that thou hast heard me. I knew that thou hearest me always, but I have said this on account of the people standing by, that they may believe..." (John 11:41-42).

Jesus did not need to write God a letter. He realized that the answer to prayer is instantaneous, that there is no need to wrestle all night or to rend one's garments. Yet, that others might understand the power of thanksgiving, he began by thanking God for hearing. He then spoke with authority: "...Lazarus, come out!" (John 11:43). And the man who had been dead did, indeed, come out of the tomb, his hands and feet still bound and his face wrapped with a cloth.

How many times have you faced what appeared to be the death of your hopes, your dreams, your deepest desires? Such a time may come at the loss of a job, the end of a marriage, the death of a loved one.

When such things occur, we can follow Jesus' example. First, we lift our eyes – we look beyond appearances to the Truth, beyond the problem to the solution. We then give thanks for the answer to our prayer. In Truth the answer is already there. Even though it has not yet manifested to our physical senses, it is there. We then speak the word with authority. We tell the Lazarus within us to come forth from the dead.

When we follow these steps in a spirit of thanksgiving, we can be as sure as Jesus that our miracle has taken place, even before we speak. We have released it to God.

Celebrate every day as if it were Thanksgiving Day, for indeed it is! Be mindful that the miracle- working power of thanksgiving is always accessible to you. It is innate in our own gracious receptivity of that which our Creator has already given us – past, present and future.

Giving thanks in advance for answered prayer is the final step in making your miracle.

Thoughts For Contemplation Or Group Discussion

1. When challenges come, we need not blame ourselves. We must look to the solution and not the challenge. If corrections are necessary, we make

these corrections while keeping our eye on the solution.
2. Giving thanks in advance for that which we desire to receive was the method of Jesus.
3. The act of giving thanks for answered prayer strengthens our faith.
4. (How do you put these rules into practice when faced with a challenge?)

Inspired Thoughts On Thanksgiving

1. "Make a joyful noise to the Lord, all the lands! Serve the Lord with gladness! Come into his presence with singing! Enter his gates with thanksgiving, and his courts with praise! Give thanks to him, bless his name!" – Psalms 100:1,2,4.
2. "…as grace extends to more and more people, it may increase thanksgiving, to the glory of God" – II Corinthians 4:16.
3. "Thanksgiving will keep the heart fresh; for true thanksgiving may be likened to rain falling upon ready soil, refreshing it and increasing its productiveness" – Charles Fillmore.

THE SIXTH LAW – THANKSGIVING

Miracles Referenced

1. Man blind from birth (John 9:1-41).
2. Geresene Demoniac (Mark 5:1-20; Matt. 8:28-34; Luke 8:26-29)
3. The 10 lepers (Luke 17:11-19)
4. Jacob (Gen. 27-33)
5. King David and depression (2 Samuel 12:15-23)
6. Multiplication of loves and fish (Matt. 14:13-23; Mark 6:30-46; Luke 9:10-17; John 6:1-16)
7. Raising Lazarus (John 11:1-12)

CHAPTER VIII

THE SEVENTH LAW – FORGIVENESS

"Forgive us our debts, as we also have forgiven our debtors..."

– Jesus (Matt. 6:12)

There are times in our lives when we have seemingly prayed without ceasing, when we have followed every guideline available, when we have persisted patiently and still the answer to our prayer does not seem to appear. We have heard the cliché, "All prayers are answered, but sometimes the answer is *no*." This is not true. God never answers *no*. God does not even know how to say *no.* We find the answer to the dilemma of seemingly unanswered prayer in the letter of James, "You ask and do not receive, because you ask wrongly…" (James 4:3).

If you have prayed, if you have followed the steps outlined, but the desired answer continues to elude you, ask yourself this question, "Is their anything that I need to forgive?" Not merely any person, but any *thing* – God, self, events, circumstances, the past, and of course, any person, as well. I am convinced that the only two things that can block the desired answer to our prayers are ignorance of how to pray, and a lack of forgiveness.

Forgiveness is simple in principle, but putting it into practice is not always so easy. I doubt that I have encountered a single counseling situation in which forgiveness would not have begun a healing of the challenge, whatever it might be. Forgiveness is the only way we can heal our relationships, our bodies and minds, and in more cases than we realize, our pocketbooks, as well.

There are three areas in which we hold grudges and need to practice forgiveness. We hold grudges against others, we hold grudges against ourselves, and we hold grudges against God.

If you are currently experiencing a challenge and really want to be rid of it, let me suggest that you closely examine yourself to see if there might be some unhappy past experience that you continue to hold against - someone or *some thing* you have failed to forgive.

We may say we have forgiven. We may even believe we have. But more often than not we are like the city dweller visiting a farm for the first time. He noted what to him appeared to be a rather strange looking cow. "Why doesn't that cow have horns?" he asked the farmer.

"Well," the farmer replied, "some cows are de-horned, and some cows are born without horns and never have 'em, and some cows shed their horns. There's lots of reasons why some cows ain't got no horns. But the reason that cow ain't got no horns is she ain't no cow. She's a mule!"

And sometimes the reason we suffer the results of not forgiving is simply because we have failed to forgive.

I mentioned that I speak from experience as a counselor of many years. I am not, however speaking from my personal experience alone. The greatest counselor was undoubtedly Jesus, and his number one topic was forgiveness.

The Greatest Counselor – Jesus

In the Sermon on the Mount (Matt. 6:6-7). Jesus said, "...if you are offering your gift at the altar, and there remember that your brother has something against you, leave your gift there before the altar and go; first be reconciled to your brother, and then come and offer your gift." (Matt. 6:23-24).

Jesus is stating that for us to pray or meditate effectively – to offer our gift to Spirit at the altar of our soul – we must first reconcile any and all negative experiences to which we are holding. We have to get *right* within ourselves.

Then Jesus goes on to say, "Make friends quickly with your accuser, while you are going with him to court, lest your accuser hand you over to the judge, and the judge to the guard, and you be put in prison; truly I say to you, you will never get out till you have paid the last penny" (Matt. 5:25-26).

This is extremely good advice on a literal level alone. We are better off to settle our disputes out of court. But if we go back and interpret what this Master Psychologist, Jesus, is really saying, we find that it goes much deeper. What Jesus is saying is that the longer we hold these grudges – whether they be grudges against another person, against our self or against God – the longer we will be imprisoned by them. From my own experience and from observing a number of suffering people, I can confidently say that there is no prison on earth that can compare with the prisons we make for ourselves.

Surely, there is no need to convince anyone reading this book that forgiveness is a good thing. Undoubtedly, you agree with this principle – at least in theory – or you would never have come so far in the study of Spiritual science. But how do we really go about putting forgiveness into practice in our lives? It is one thing to understand in theory, another to practice it.

Forgive Others

Imagine this situation: you have been hurt. Some person or group of persons that you have truly cared for and trusted has disappointed you, perhaps even deceived you. The human response is to get even in the deadliest way possible. This is the human way, the way that "turns us over to the judge, and the judge to the guard and the guard to the prison." And Jesus tells us we are not released until we pay the last penny – the law of cause and effect.

But there is a higher law that Jesus taught, a law that supersedes the law of cause and effect. That law is *grace*, and, as Jesus taught it, *grace* and *forgiveness* are almost synonymous.

Let us return to our imaginary scenario. You were hurt. You were cut to the quick. Why should you give him/her/them the satisfaction of forgiveness? That person who hurt you does not deserve forgiveness, does he?

The paradoxical Truth is that when we forgive, we do it for ourselves, not for anyone else. Let me repeat that, and I hope you will etch it in big, bold letters in your heart and soul. YOU ARE PRACTICING FORGIVENESS, NOT FOR THE SAKE OF YOUR OFFENDER, BUT IN ORDER TO BE FREE YOURSELF!!!

Lack of forgiveness literally changes the chemistry in the body and brain. It depletes the immune system. It causes arthritis, cancer, mental illness and who knows what else. It destroys prosperity and plays havoc with relationships.

Is getting even with the person who hurt you worth paying that price? Your pain and suffering bothers him or her not one iota. He may not even be aware of it. He just goes along his merry way, enjoying life, while you sit in a dark brown fog, holding your grudge and turning into a sour pickle. This is what happens to people who refuse to forgive. Did you know that? They turn into a symbolic, warty, sour pickle.

So first of all, recognize that forgiving that other person is for the purpose of setting *you* free – letting *you* out of prison. Forgiveness is the ultimate act of Selfishness – *Selfishness* spelled with a capital *S* – the kind of *Selfishness* that helps you become the person you were created to be.

Nor need you concern yourself that Spiritual law is not at work. You can be assured that a Higher Power than you is teaching your offender his or her lesson!

What He Did Is Unforgivable!!!

Another argument against forgiving is that what that person did is unforgivable.

Remember this: forgiveness does not imply agreement. It does not mean you condone a particular action. You may never agree that what took place was correct or just. This is not necessary. Forced forgiveness is very shallow and rarely lasting. True forgiveness requires much less energy. True forgiveness is simply turning loose of the hold an experience has on you. It is releasing the pain that *you* feel.

Again, hear Jesus on this point. He had called his disciples together and was advising them on how to proceed in their ministry:

> ...whatever town or village you enter find out who is worthy in it, and stay with him until you depart. As you enter the house, salute it. And if the house is worthy, let your peace come upon it,

but if it is not worthy, let you peace return to you. And if any one will not receive you or listen to your words, shake off the dust from your feet as you leave that house or town.

(Matt. 10:11-14)

"Shake the dust from your feet!" Do not carry even a grain of that experience with you! Who suffered when Jesus left a town? Certainly it was not Jesus or his disciples. They just went their way, sharing their message of God's love and wholeness with those who listened. Those who suffered were the people who would not listen. They were the ones who were not healed. They were the ones who were not prospered. They were the ones without love in their hearts.

The People Of Nazareth (Mark 6:1-6)

Can you imagine Jesus' withholding forgiveness? As a human being there were surely times when he experienced hurt. For example the story is told of his entering his hometown of Nazareth to teach in the synagogue.

Do you recall how he was received? Did they give him a key to the city? Hire a band and cater a banquet?

Quite the opposite! They said, "Isn't this the carpenter's son? Isn't his mother called 'Mary'? And aren't his brothers James and Joseph and Simon and Judas? And aren't his sisters with us? Where then did this man get all this?"

In other words, "This is 'Old Bubba' from 'Boggy Bluff.' Just who does he think he is?"

Jesus' response is classic: "A prophet is not without honor except in his own country and in his own house." And we read: "...he could do no mighty work there, except that he laid his hands upon a few sick people and healed them. And he marveled because of their unbelief."

But note: Even in the midst of this most negative of environments, he healed *some* of the people.

We might think, "Well, of course Jesus could shake away the dust of disappointment and move on. He was *different*; he was *Jesus!*"

But who was Jesus? Jesus of Nazareth was a human being, just as you and I are human beings. He had parents and brothers and sisters. He ate and slept just as we do. He felt pain, both physically and emotionally.

But there was a difference. Jesus so believed in the love of God and humankind and their Oneness that his true Self shone through. And when this happened there was no longer a separation between the human being, Jesus of Nazareth and Jesus, the Christ. Jesus is our Example, our Elder Brother, our Wayshower. And Jesus, himself, told us that everything he did, we could do also (John 13:12). Even become a Christ!

Shall we attempt to understand how Jesus was able to walk away from the disappointment, the embarrassment, the hurt of being snubbed, cut down by his own neighbors in Nazareth? He did it by keeping his eyes on the goal, rather than allowing himself to become distracted by the little periphery goings-on.

Look at this all-too-familiar example and see how Jesus' technique would work. A husband and wife are having trouble, perhaps a separation or divorce has taken place. They begin to play the game of *Gotcha!* You know who the pawns are in this game – the children, of course, and this is a game passed on for generations.

How much better it would be to focus on the good qualities of the other individual, despite grievances, instead of focusing attention on his or her flaws and thinking up ways to get even! A child's own self-esteem is influenced greatly by how he or she sees a parent through the eyes of the other parent, as well as the opinions of trusted family and friends. Children sense these feelings inherently. How does it make a child feel to be told constantly how worthless her own parent is? Instinctively, we know that we are a part of that parent and some of that assumed worthlessness reflects on us. Much emotional pain and sickness results from absorbing these attitudes. As human beings we *need* to feel that our fathers and mothers are persons of value.

How much better it would be to focus love on the children, on making sure they remain secure and filled with self-respect and do not suffer as a result of the adult's personal challenges! The children would surely gain a greater sense of self-worth, and the possibility even exists that the marriage may be saved, or at least a friendship salvaged.

Regardless, there are no winners in the game of *Gotcha!* Everybody loses!

Another example: A co-worker has offended you, or is not doing his or her share of the work, or whatever. There are many variations on this theme.

How much better it would be to focus that energy on doing the best job possible, rather than looking for ways to play *Gotcha! By* doing your best, you may be promoted away from that other person. Or by removing your focus from the unpleasant incident, you may discover that the entire episode was only a misunderstanding and your friendship may be restored. Or a new friendship may have begun. At the very least, by doing your best, you have helped the economy!

On the other hand, when we allow an incident to fester and grow, everybody loses.

To forgive others, regardless of the challenge, we must realize that whatever mistake was made, it was made out of ignorance. Can you accept that? It is always true, even in the case of a *Hitler*.

This may be a difficult, perhaps even shocking concept. "Why, of course they knew what they were doing!" you might say. But the Truth remains that *everyone* is doing the best he or she can at their current level of understanding. If they *could* do better, they *would* do better. No one sets out to be evil. *Evil* is simply the false belief that we can be separated from our good or God, and no one with even a grain of understanding would want that. That we are doing the best we can at our current level of understanding is a basic principle of Spiritual law.

Unfortunately, many set out with a total lack of awareness of the workings of this Law, and inevitably, they pay a very high price.

The ultimate in forgiveness is exemplified by Jesus, when he prayed from the cross, "Father, forgive them, for they know not what they do" (John 23:34).

Has anyone strung you up to a cross lately? It is pretty bad. There is a great deal of physical pain involved in a crucifixion, not to mention the mental and emotional anguish. And death does not come swiftly.

But if our Example could forgive in such a situation, should we not at least give some consideration to forgiving the little slights we experience?

This does not mean you should take that person who offended you and make him or her your best friend. When Jesus appeared after the resurrection, it was not to the Pharisees and others involved in his persecution – nor did he appear to Judas. In their state of consciousness, they most likely would never have even recognized him. Jesus appeared to his disciples and to Mary Magdalene and the other Mary. And he prepared food for them (John 21:4-12). Metaphysically, he gave them Spiritual nourishment.

Forgive Yourself

But assume you have taken that giant leap and forgiven even your worst critic. Very likely, you still have a long way to go.

Consider this: how completely have you forgiven yourself? Forgiving others is a great deal easier than forgiving oneself. Even the most loving among us can be very hard on their self.

Again, be aware that any mistake you made was only that, a mistake made out of ignorance. This is true even if you think you knew better. Knowing with the *head* and knowing with the *heart* can be two very different things. With today's understanding, would you repeat that error? If not, the error is removed. *Grace* has intervened – the realization that you have grown to a point where you *could not* knowingly make that mistake again.

So realize that the "you" who made that error no longer exists. And how long can you continue to blame a person who does not exist?

The Paralytic

Do you recall the story we examined earlier about the paralytic who was carried by four men and let down through the roof of a house in order to see Jesus and be healed? (Mark 2:1-12; Matt. 9:2-8; Luke 6:17-26). Apparently, Jesus perceived the guilt he felt regarding something in his past. Jesus spoke to the man as he lay on the pallet, "My son, your sins are forgiven," he told him.

Immediately, the scribes in attendance took issue. They began questioning, "Why does this man (Jesus) speak thus? It is blasphemy! Who can forgive sins but God alone?"

THE SEVENTH LAW – FORGIVENESS

Perhaps we will understand the scribe better and perhaps even feel less harshly toward him if we consider the work in which he was engaged. Since printing presses were not invented until hundreds of years after Jesus' birth, all written material came to the people of that day as a result of the work of the Scribes. They were men who patiently and meticulously copied the scriptures by hand, when extra copies were needed and when older copies were too worn to be read any longer.

The Scribe was extraordinarily meticulous in making exact copies. It took a very special type of person to even take on such a job. If he made even a single error in writing, it was often necessary that he destroy the entire sheet of precious papyrus or vellum and start again from the beginning. After he finished copying a particular book, the Scribe would then count each word and letter contained within it to determine that it match the one from which he had been copying to prove that no error had been made. We can clearly see that this was not a job for just anyone!

It is probably safe to say that Scribes were men who were totally dedicated to the letter of the law. To them, and other religious leaders of that day, it was essential that the letter of the law be observed. Metaphysically, we might think of them as symbolizing thoughts that come to us from the outer world, as opposed to Spirit's inward inspiration. We can see by the comments of the scribes when Jesus healed the paralytic that they were much more concerned with the legal ramifications of the event than with the condition of the man.

Jesus was totally familiar with the *scribal mentality* and he easily recognized their thought process. "Why do you question thus in your hearts?" he asked them. "Which is easier, to say to the paralytic, 'Your sins are forgiven,' or to say, 'Rise, take up you pallet and walk'?" Then, so that the Scribes, locked in their literal-mindedness, would not fail to understand, he said directly to them, "But that you may know that the Son of man has authority on earth to forgive sins," he turned to the paralytic and continued, "I say to you, rise, take up your pallet and go home."

The man who had been paralyzed did as Jesus told him, and we read that everyone was amazed and glorified God saying, "We never saw anything like this!"

Withholding forgiveness is painful. Holding a grudge against oneself can be paralyzing. Yet within our consciousness there may be *Scribes* who insist that our sin is unforgivable, that only God *out there* has the right to offer absolution. The Christ within knows this as a part of human nature and is constantly saying to us, "Your sins are forgiven. Turn loose of them. Let them go. Now get up, and do the things that need to be done by you!"

Correct That Error

If you are experiencing guilt because of some past error, if you possibly can, correct the error. Make physical restitution where possible. Tell that friend that you acted out of ignorance and regret any pain or inconvenience your ignorance may have brought about.

There are times, however, when restitution is not possible or even advisable. We should never attempt to soothe our own conscience at someone else's expense. Confession may be good for the soul, but we should not seek this good for oneself, while bringing pain to another.

Nevertheless, if confession is not appropriate or possible, you can still correct the mistake and forgive yourself. Within your own consciousness during a time of meditation, mentally talk with the person or persons who may have been involved, the persons you feel you may have wronged and even the persons who may have wronged you.

If you are feeling pain in your soul for any reason whatsoever, you especially need to do this.

Create a comfortable setting for yourself, and visualize or sense that person sitting beside you. Allow yourself to speak directly from your heart. Tell him or her that you made mistakes in judgment. But keep in mind that there is no need for justification. This exercise is to cleanse your soul, not to corroborate your right to be angry. Have a real heart-to-heart conversation with that person or persons – for the purpose of freeing yourself.

If you are not good at visualization or if you feel this time of contemplation could degenerate into something other than a cleansing session, I mentioned a technique in a previous chapter that is very effective for me – that of writing a letter.

Sit down and write a letter to anyone who was involved in this painful situation. Or write it to God or your own Higher Self or *their* Higher Self. Write it over and over till the words you express are precisely what your soul longs to say.

It is good to go through a cleansing process such as this every day, rather than allowing mistakes to fester. An effective way to cleanse oneself of these little day-to-day mistakes is to spend a time at the end of each day simply reliving its experiences. If a memory pops up that you feel uncomfortable with, take it out and examine it. Then within your powerful faculty of imagination literally change the area in which you misrepresented yourself.

The truth is that your subjective mind does not know the difference between a factual experience and one you have vividly imaged. So relive that experience, making any change you choose in your responses. We may not be able to change others, but we can change our own reaction to that experience and when we do that, the real miracle occurs. We find the outer experience changes accordingly.

We have looked at techniques and Jesus' example in forgiving others and ourselves. But what about those grudges we sometimes hold against God?

Does that shock you? Have you never held a grudge against God?

Let me assure you that most of us have. Some examples: Have you ever felt that life is not fair? Bad luck plagues you... You never get the breaks... Perhaps you are *accident-prone* or come from a *dysfunctional family*... Parents used to tell their children that they (the parent) walked twenty miles to school in five feet of snow, back and forth – barefoot! Today we come from *dysfunctional* families.

The Man By The Pool (John 5:1-16)

Do you recall the lame man who sat by the pool of Bethzatha for thirty-eight years? The belief was that the first person who entered the pool when the waters stirred would be healed.

Jesus asked him, "Do you *want* to be healed?" Instead of a direct *yes* or *no* answer, the man began to enumerate the manner in which he was mistreated each time the waters stirred: no one would help him, they jumped in front of him. He was deeply enmeshed in self-pity, which is simply another name for anger at God.

We can almost imagine Jesus' frustration as he told him, "Rise, take up you pallet and walk." This must have been exactly what the man needed to hear, for we read that he did exactly as Jesus told him and was healed.

This was the Sabbath, and there were Jews near the pool who observed what was taking place. Metaphysically, *Jews* represent thoughts and feelings that at least have been exposed to things of a spiritual nature. But these *Jews* were officials in the synagogues and Temple, and their attitude was one of extreme dogmatism. They approached the newly healed man, not to discuss his healing, but ridiculously enough, to debate the pros and cons of his carrying a pallet on the Sabbath. They then interrogated him at length, regarding who was responsible for this healing. Finally, they departed, leaving him in the Temple, surrounded by a teeming crowd of noisy disbelievers.

Jesus later found him there and assured him, "See, you are well! Sin no more, that nothing worse befall you."

When we attempt to heal our misconceptions of life and God, we may well discover Pharisaical aspects within our own minds that emerge to question the rightness or wrongness of our newfound beliefs. Frequently, they are old religious teachings and they may appear in the guise of family members, longtime friends, even memories of social events treasured for years. They swarm out of the unconscious race mind and would have us remain in an *in-valid* state, rather than allow us to rise and challenge the status quo. These questionings invariably leave us in a crowded, confused condition, surrounded by self-disapproval as was the case of the man in the Temple.

But the Christ invariably seeks us out in our Temple and reminds us, "See, you are well. You are a different person than before! Release those erroneous beliefs about God and life. Turn loose of them, so that nothing worse befalls you."

Forgive God

When we complain about things like life's being unfair, or the conditions in which we were born, or diseases we had, or fate, or luck, or the stars, or karma, or kismet; Who or What are we angry with, if not God?

But even more important, how do we start to forgive God? We might begin by realizing that we are all in the same boat. Everyone faces challenges, not the same challenges, but challenges, nevertheless. It is part of the human condition. And if all those challenges were put in a bag and mixed up, you would probably choose the same old familiar challenges.

The truth is that you were not singled out by a capricious fate to be picked on, and there is no point in any of us playing a game of Cosmic one-upmanship. The important thing is not how badly we were hurt or mistreated. The only way to be made whole is to look away from the challenge and forward to the solution.

We begin this process by realizing that God or that Power which created the universe and everything in it knows nothing about sin, punishment or forgiveness. If God knew of sin, then evil would be a reality. Each day, affirm this Truth: *There is only one Presence and one Power in the Universe and in my individual world, and that Presence and that Power is God, and God is Absolute Goodness!*

Absolute goodness... Contemplate the word, *absolute*. Can Absolute Goodness have any comprehension of evil? Think about it. If Absolute Goodness perceived evil. It would not be Absolute Goodness.

If we can accept this, then God must be absolved of all blame for anything painful that has ever occurred in our lives. Can you do that? Recognize that God does not now, never has and never will bring pain into your life for any reason whatsoever.

Let us examine another premise – that evil is only ignorance of Truth. We have touched on this before, but it is so important that it bears repeating. Evil has no principle behind it, as goodness does. If it did, mistakes could never be corrected. We might compare *evil or ignorance* to a darkened room. When we turn a light on, the darkness disappears. The darkness does not huddle in ugly little globs in the corners. The darkness is simply illumined (removed) by the light.

The same is true for the pain we suffer in life. In some way, it is a natural consequence of breaking Spiritual Law, it is a symptom, a reminder that we are making a mistake that needs to be corrected. Life never punishes! But life offers many gentle (and some not-so-gentle) reminders that we have made errors that need correcting. We need not feel guilty. The only purpose for these reminders is to enable us to live the more abundant life!

This is the value of forgiveness. It is the most effective way to get back in tune with the Infinite, the most efficient way to make a miracle – forgiving others for expressing less than perfection, forgiving ourselves for the times we fall short, forgiving Life for the pain our own misconceptions have brought us. When we recognize that everyone has suffered in one way or another, that we have not been singled out as some kind of cosmic stepchild, then we can get on with the business of healing ourselves and others and loving ourselves back into our Divinity. When we do this, we have begun our move from the human to the Divine, and our miracle is in the making.

Thoughts For Contemplation Or Group Discussion

Lack of forgiveness can be a major block to answered prayer.

1. We practice forgiveness of others in order to free ourselves.
2. Forgiveness does not imply agreement.
3. We should correct mistakes we have made whenever possible.
4. We must forgive ourselves for mistakes made, because we are no longer the same person who made them.
5. We must release any belief that we have been singled out to suffer.
6. Forgiveness, grace and release may be considered synonymous.
7. God loves us.

    (Do you agree with these statements? If not, explain why. If so, share how you have come to this understanding.)

Inspired Thoughts About Forgiveness

1. "...forgive us our sins, for we ourselves forgive everyone who is indebted to us..." – Jesus (Luke: 11:4).

2. "For thou, O Lord, art good and forgiving, Abounding in steadfast love to all who call on thee" – Psalms 86:5.
3. "We read that we ought to forgive our enemies; but we do not read that we ought to forgive our friends" – attributed to Cosmus, Duke of Florence, by Bacon.
4. "His heart was as great as the world, but there was no room in it to hold the memory of a wrong" – Emerson.
5. "I pardon him, as God shall pardon me" – Shakespeare, (Richard II).
6. "To err is human; to forgive, divine" – Pope.

Miracles Referenced

1. Healing – The people of Nazareth (Mark 6:1-6)
2. Healing – The paralytic (Mark 2:1-12; Matthew 9:2-8; Luke 6:17-26)
3. Healing – The man by the pool (John 6:1-16)

CHAPTER IX

THE MIRACLE MODEL

"And all ate and were satisfied. And they took up what was left over, twelve baskets of broken pieces"

(Luke 9:17).

Only one miracle performed by Jesus is told in all four Gospels. Very few events in his life are told by each of the writers. Some are told in one Gospel account, stressing a particular viewpoint; others are told twice, with a probable common source. A number of Jesus' miracles are reported in each of the three synoptic gospels, Matthew, Mark and Luke, with Mark's earliest version, written about 65 to 70 AD, as their most likely source. Some personal elaborations and information were doubtlessly added by each of the writers.

Of the miracles recorded by the writer of the Gospel of John, only the miracle of the feeding of the five thousand is told by the other three Gospel writers, and the story is told by each of them, not so much from a unique point of view, but with such similarity in the steps Jesus took that they can easily be outlined. This perfect pattern for prayer becomes the miracle model for those who are willing to seek out the deeper meanings in its message.

The Death Of John The Baptist

The background for this miracle is a dramatic one. It begins in the three Synoptic Gospels with the story of the beheading of John the Baptizer by the Jewish king, Herod Antipas (Matthew 14:1-12; Mark 6:14-29; Luke 9:7-9). As you probably recall, the king gave a banquet for his courtiers and officers to celebrate his birthday. During the festivities, his stepdaughter danced for Herod and his guests and pleased the king so greatly that he told her, "Ask me whatever you wish, and I will grant it."

Apparently, the girl was an obedient daughter, for she went directly to her mother, Herodias, to determine what this very important request should be. Without hesitation, her mother replied, "The head of John the Baptizer!" (Mark 6:24).

Herodias' prompt reply would certainly indicate that John was not one of her favorite people, and with good reason. Prior to his imprisonment, John had taken it upon himself to go about the country, vehemently denouncing her marriage to King Herod as incestuous (Leviticus 18:16, 20, 21). (Herodias was not only the former wife of Herod's half-brother, her own biological uncle Philip, but was Herod's half-niece as well. Her father, Aristobulus and Herod Antipas were sons of the paranoid Herod the Great, who, imagining ever-present conspiracies, had Aristobulus executed. To complicate matters, Herod had divorced his previous wife to marry Herodias. With such a background we can see why the vindictive Herodias wanted nothing more than to permanently still the accusing tongue of John the Baptist.)

King Herod was well aware of the precarious position in which granting the girl's request placed him. John the Baptist was extremely popular with the people, and Herod was hated. First of all, he was a half-breed. While his father had been of Jewish parentage, his mother was a Samaritan, a racially obnoxious group to Jewish nationalists. Such prejudice would be considered *politically incorrect* today, but to the Jews of that time it was very real and acceptable. Second, there was little sympathy for such *dysfunctional* families as the Herod clan, with their incestuous marriages, divorces, remarriages and murders. Finally, and this would have been sufficient in itself, Herod was considered a puppet of Roman rule.

Though Herod had dared to imprison John, he fully recognized the dangers inherent in the execution of so popular a personage. Nevertheless, he felt impelled to keep his word to this stepdaughter/grand-niece in order that he not lose face before his guests. Thus, John was beheaded and his head placed on a platter and given to the girl, who proudly presented it to her mother.

We can safely assume that the death of John the Baptist was not a *high point* in Jesus' life or ministry. First of all, John was a close friend and associate of Jesus, perhaps even his cousin. It was John who baptized Jesus at the beginning of his ministry and was the first to recognize his unparalleled potential. Surely, Jesus felt a personal loss and even shock at so cruel and grizzly an ending to a great life.

This was not likely the only reason that John's death was a blow to Jesus on a very human, personal level. It vividly pointed out the precarious nature of his own ministry, indeed, of his own life.

A Banquet For Five Thousand

The Gospel of Matthew begins the story by saying, "Now when Jesus heard of this (referring to John's beheading) he withdrew from there in a boat to a lonely place apart..." It is at this point that the story of the *feeding of the five thousand* begins (Mark 6:30-44; Matthew 14:13-21; Luke 9:10-17; John 6:1-13). This is Mark's version:

> And he (Jesus) said to them, "Come away by yourselves to a lonely place, and rest a while." For many were coming and going, and they had no leisure even to eat. And they went away in the boat to a lonely place by themselves. Now many saw them going, and knew them, and they ran there on foot from all the towns, and got there ahead of them. As he went ashore he saw a great throng, and he had compassion on them, because they were like sheep without a shepherd; and he began to teach them many things. And when it grew late, his disciples came to him and said, "This is a lonely place, and the hour is now late; send them away, to go into the country and villages round about and buy themselves something to eat." But Jesus answered them, "You give them something to eat." and they said to him, "Shall we go and

buy two hundred denarii worth of bread, and give it to them to eat?" And he said to them, "How many loaves have you? Go and see." And when they had found out, they said, "Five, and two fish." Then he commanded them all to sit down by companies upon the green grass. So they sat down in groups, by hundreds and by fifties. And taking the five loaves and the two fish he looked up to heaven, and blessed and broke the loaves, and gave them to the disciples to set before the people; and he divided the two fish among them all. And they all ate and were satisfied. And they took up twelve basketsful of broken pieces and the fish. And those who ate the loaves were five thousand men.

My research in numerous Bible commentaries regarding this very important miracle has yielded very little light on the process by which this multiplication of food took place. Strangely enough, I found this to be a theologically controversial miracle. One scholarly explanation states, "…that others besides the disciples had brought their provision with them, and that what Jesus achieved was to get a mixed multitude to pool its resources and those who had food to share with those who lacked." This is an appealing explanation, in no way offensive. To change a group of grasping, self-centered mortals, greedily clinging to every morsel of bread into cooperating, sharing human beings is no small miracle in itself!

Generally speaking, however, the consensus of most Biblical commentaries follows one of these two points: first, there is no historical basis to believe that Jesus' multiplication of bread and fish took place at all; or second, if it did, it was done to prove Jesus' difference from ordinary humankind and has little value in our lives today. (Same old story!) Faced with these two (to me) very unsatisfactory choices, I turn to the more spiritual, metaphysical approach.

Personal Transformation

The story of the feeding of the five thousand is not only the miracle model for demonstrating health, prosperity, loving relationships and all the good of life, but it is also the formula for transforming ourselves from the *five sense human being* into a true *Spiritual being.*

Can anything less than this be the greatest of miracles?

As we examine this model, remember to consider each character, each place, and each event as taking place within, rather than an event occurring in a distant time and place, involving a group of unnamed, hungry people *out there*. The Bible is *your personal story!*

This miracle begins with the beheading of Jesus' friend, John the Baptist. John signifies an *intellectual perception of Truth, not fully spiritualized.* John represents that state of mind that seeks zealously for the rule of Spirit and sees it as a possibility, but not an experienced reality.

Surely, we see ourselves in John. He insisted that others change their outer behavior. Have you ever observed this in yourself? Most of us probably have. John's condemnation of King Herod and Herodias brought about the loss of his head. This in no way justifies Herod's actions, though it does illustrate a spiritual point: change must come from within ourselves. As the song goes, "Let there be peace on earth, and let it begin with me."

This was not John's way. His message was "Repent!" and we might add, "And do it my way!!!" John's was an attitude still striving with evil as reality, not yet discerning that only Truth has power. This attitude must be decapitated from our consciousness, as the story of John the Baptist so vividly portrays. The belief in evil as a reality must literally be severed from our mind.

Unfortunately, many of us enter the study of Truth carrying with us a *John the Baptist* state of mind. We see Truth as a beautiful ideal and simply cannot understand why everyone else does not perceive it *exactly* as we do.

We may become *instant evangelists,* assuming that others are just waiting with bated breath for us to impart our new-found wisdom, which we more than gladly do.

In my very early days of studying Truth, it came as a real shock to discover that my friends and extended family members were not waiting for *anything* I had to say regarding metaphysics or anything else that challenged the status quo. I found that they would, in fact, rather not hear anything about it, though they were more than happy to point out any fallacies from their strictly fundamentalist point of view. It was obvious that their minds were *not* going to be changed and my efforts were simply an exercise in futility pursued for my own benefit, not theirs.

Eventually, *my* need to convince the world diminished.

Metaphysical Honeymoons

This *evangelical* period may be likened to a *metaphysical honeymoon.* Fortunately, most of us eventually relax and settle into a *happy marriage* with Truth, realizing that the world has all of eternity to gain this great knowledge and it is perfectly all right for us to simply *let* it happen – by example, rather than oration.

The *John the Baptist mentality,* however, is not satisfied with this. It feels compelled to correct the log in a neighbor's eye and is even willing to denounce the ills of the entire world. Quite an undertaking!

This *head trip* must, by its very nature, come to an end; thus, the symbolic beheading of John. Nevertheless, the human part of us mourns such passing.

Facing Challenges

There is another point of view which the beheading of John the Baptist represents in our lives, that of facing major challenges. This need not be the case, yet too often we fail to turn to Spirit until forced to do so through pain and suffering of one kind or another.

When Jesus faced this situation (the very gruesome death of John), we are told that "many were coming and going, and they had no leisure even to eat."

Have you ever faced a difficult situation – a life change so momentous that it seemed a beheading? I vividly recall such a time in my own life. I was about sixteen and had just begun college when I was faced with a decision that would affect my entire future. I had to decide whether to continue school or drop out for a time (perhaps forever) because my father had been diagnosed with an incurable condition.

I slept very little that night. My father was extremely dear to me and the pain at the thought of losing him was overwhelming. On top of that I was forced to rethink every plan I had taken for granted for a lifetime. Never had the possibility of postponing college even occurred to me.

Let me assure you that many frightening thoughts and feelings were *coming and going* through my mind that night. When I finally fell into a fitful sleep of some sort, I dreamed that my body was being dismembered, bit by bit.

This is a gory illustration, I know, but the Bible is no less graphic in its depictions of our troubled emotional states. These are universal symbols, common to each of us.

At that time I was not familiar with Truth teachings. The physician's prognosis was the equivalent of God's. I had no concept of Spiritual healing. And my concept of prayer was probably that if I pleaded convincingly enough, God might take pity on me and change His mind, spare my father and somehow work things out without troubling me. This did not happen.

Prayer

As you see, mine was not a very enlightened outlook and my understanding of prayer was crude, so the terrors that inhabit the unillumined consciousness continued *coming and going, and I had no leisure.*

But Jesus understood what to do when faced with traumatic events. Surely he did not plead with God, nor even lose a moment's sleep. Jesus knew that it was not beneficial to remain in a state of consciousness devoid of spiritual nourishment. Immediately, he set about to change *his* state of mind. He said to his disciples, "Come away by yourselves to a lonely place and rest a while." In other words, "This is not a good *place* to be. It's time to practice relaxation and meditation and change our consciousness so we can get on with our lives." And we read that "...they went away in a boat to a lonely place by themselves."

A Boat Ride To Bethsaida

A *boat* represents a state of consciousness that protects one from sinking into the depths of depression and loss. It is similar to the *room* Jesus spoke of when he said, "...when you pray, go into your room and shut the door and pray to your Father who is in secret; and your Father who sees in secret will reward you" (Matthew 6:6).

When events in our outer world, whatever they might be, disturb the peace of our souls, this is what we must do. We must enter our little boat, (our room), and "come away by ourselves to a lonely place and rest a while." This is a very important step in making that miracle!

THE MIRACLE MODEL

Luke, in telling of this incident, is more specific than Mark and Matthew. He states: "And he (Jesus) took them (the disciples) and withdrew apart to a city called Bethsaida." In other words, Jesus left Galilee, *the activity of life on the human plane* and moved to the city of Bethsaida, meaning *house of fishing, place of nets, fishing town*. Since *fish* refer to *spiritual ideas,* we see that Jesus was in the process of raising his consciousness from that of loss, symbolized by John's death, to that of multiplication and increase of creative, Spiritual ideas.

From a totally literal point of view, such a move was a very wise one on Jesus' part. The city of Bethsaida is north of the Sea of Galilee and east of the place where the Jordan River enters. The Jordan River was the boundary of Galilee; thus, Bethsaida was not in Galilee, ruled by the murderous Herod Antipas, but in the province of Iturea. By making this move, Jesus was removing himself from Herod Antipas' jurisdiction to that of the less treacherous Philip the Tetrarch. Thus, the clear message; move from a state of consciousness ruled by fear and infamy to one of greater serenity and peace, even if that state of mind does not yet express its maximum spiritual capacity.

When Jesus approached the other shore (when he moved from one state of consciousness to another), people from all the nearby towns rushed to meet him and a great throng awaited his arrival. We read that Jesus had compassion on them and began to teach them many things (Matt. 14:13-15).

In our personal lives we might equate this to times when we begin the process of moving from a negative state of mind to a higher level. Perhaps we seek a healing, a prospering, a harmonizing of a relationship. At such times, we are frequently aware of great throngs of thoughts and feelings rushing in on us – old beliefs, old attitudes, outmoded ways of looking at life.

We must remember that this throng rushes to us, not to harm us, but to be fed (spiritually nourished), to be instructed in Truth and healed of erroneous beliefs. In the silence we allow Truth to speak through us and teach these spiritually unillumined thoughts and feelings. This Christ Wisdom is always within, seeking the receptive mind and heart. Truth teaches and faith hears.

Let Them Eat Cake!

As the day passed and it grew late, Jesus' disciples came to him and suggested that since it was so late and they were in a lonely place, they should send the people into the nearby country and villages to buy food for themselves. But Jesus responded to this suggestion by saying," *You* give them something to eat." Jesus made a personal commitment.

When we have prayed and meditated, diligently seeking the answer to a challenge or seeking that elusive sense of peace, certain aspects within us, represented here by the disciples, might tell us, "Hey, we're hungry. This is all very nice and we appreciate your good thoughts and pleasant remarks, but really – what we need now is a miracle! Maybe the psychic on the corner or that "channeler" I've been reading about. Or even a good stiff drink might help!"

In a word, we are often tempted to seek our spiritual nourishment outside of the one place where it can be found – within. At such a time, the indwelling Christ speaks to our spiritual faculties: "*You* give them something to eat!"

The disciples then asked Jesus, "Shall we go and buy two hundred denarii worth of bread and give it to them...?" A denarius was a full day's wage for a laborer, so we can see that his disciples were saying, "How in the world do you expect us to feed all these people? What do you think we're made of – *money?*"

Again, they thought only to seek their good in the outer, rather than from within.

But Jesus replied, "How many loaves have you? Go and see." In other words, "Stop complaining and looking to the outer and discover what resources you *already* have."

The disciples did as they were told and reported to Jesus that they had five loaves of bread and two fish. Not a lot, but at least a beginning.

The Significance Of Numbers

As stated earlier, in metaphysical interpretation each word is significant, especially numbers. Numerology was an important part of mystical Judaism, and the writers of the scriptures, as well as Jesus, were well versed in it. As we read the Bible, certain numbers are used repeatedly, and these are as much a part of the mystical code as names of places and people are. The secret meanings contained in these numbers are very logical and easily understood.

The number *five* is a particularly important number. It generally refers to our *five physical senses* – sight, hearing, smell, taste and touch. *Bread* represents *universal substance,* that *spiritual essence* out of which everything is first brought into being. The five loaves refer to the involvement of our five physical senses in spiritual substance – substance being that which stands under all form. Five loaves of bread represent the activity of the imagination In the process of creation.

You need not fret or even concern yourself over how this takes place.

Whatever your need or desire might be – peace of mind, an expanded ability to love, a forgiving heart, a stronger faith, or something more tangible – your job is to *image* the *completed result* as a reality NOW. It is not to determine how that end result will come into being, but simply *what* is to be. Your subjective mind is an ever-alert servant that knows how to bring all things into being. It will guide you to the information you need, to the right persons and places that will assist you, to innumerable seeming *coincidences that* bring your miracle into being. Trust it!

Only your *conscious mind* can impress this servant with the image of what to create. This is done by visualizing the completed picture as clearly as possible, hearing the sounds associated with its successful completion, being aware of any tastes or aromas that would be a part of this happy scene, as well as the feel or taste or touch of objects. Then add to this all of the good emotions that would be a part of having achieved this desired goal. It is through the imagination that we create the *feeling that* our goal is completed *now,* and it is this *feeling* that is most important.

As noted before, *fish* refer to *ideas,* and in this case there were two fish. The number *two* represents our ability to say *yes* and *no,* to *affirm* and *deny.* We affirm that which we wish to build up – that we are happy, loving, prosperous, healthy children of God – and we deny that which we wish to dissolve from our consciousness and consequently from our experience. It is through the process of affirming and denying that we convince our *thinking nature* that our goal *is* accomplished, thus freeing it to *be* accomplished.

When the thinking and feeling natures are in agreement, a mystical marriage takes place in mind. The goal has been accepted by the feminine or feeling nature and by the masculine or thinking nature. When this is achieved, your good is not only conceived, but the spiritual pattern has become a reality long before it appears in visible form. *Thinking* and *feeling* make it so.

Jesus then told the people to sit by companies on the grass. He took the five loaves and the two fish and looked up to heaven, then blessed and broke the loaves and gave them to the disciples to set before the people. With only two fish and five loaves in his hand, Jesus gave thanks for his answered prayer (food to feed five thousand people). This power of thanksgiving is the catalyst that brings spiritual nourishment into being. And we are told that all ate and were satisfied, and the disciples took up twelve baskets-full of broken pieces of bread and fish.

The Model

In Jesus' *miracle model we* see the steps he used in bringing that spiritual pattern into being:

First, regardless of the seeming challenge, Jesus began with a relaxed state of mind. He told his disciples (spiritual faculties), "Come away by yourselves to a lonely place and rest awhile."

Meditate. Pray.

Second, he made a personal commitment; he told his disciples, "*You* give them something to eat."

Talk to your fears, doubts, concerns until they are convinced that all is well.

Third, Jesus expressed faith. Even in the face of lack, he looked away from seeming limitation toward the resources that were available. He asked his disciples, "How many loaves have you? Go and see." Then, like the proverbial optimist who prays for rain and actually carries an umbrella, Jesus had the crowd sit down to prepare for dining.

Take that giant step of seeing yourself as you want to be.

Fourth, Jesus looked up to heaven and blessed the food that they had. He recognized God as its only Source and gave thanks in advance for his answered prayer.

Fifth, Jesus broke the five loaves. He activated the power inherent in the imagination – the five physical senses interfacing with Spiritual substance. He had done his work; now he allowed Spirit to do Its work.

Begin to act as if you were *already* the person you long to be.

Sixth, he divided the two fish among the people. He utilized the power of affirmations and denials to bring about a change in his multitude of spiritually hungry thoughts and feelings.

Affirm that your prayer is answered now. Deny any false belief to the contrary.

And last, he released it to God.

Let go and let God bring your answered prayer into being.

Leftovers

The most marvelous part of this story is that everyone ate and was satisfied.

When we search for our good in the outer world, we are never satisfied. As soon as we achieve one success, we seek another; but when we partake of spiritual nourishment provided by our indwelling Christ, we eat and we remain satisfied.

After the meal the disciples took up twelve baskets-full of broken pieces of bread and fish. The number *twelve* refers to *spiritual fulfillment*.

The story concludes by reiterating that "...those who ate...were five thousand men." In other words, by following Jesus' pattern, the five-sense man or woman is *Spiritually* satisfied. And the good news is that there is no depletion of that spiritual good. We are able to partake of this limitless bounty as often as we choose, and an infinity remains.

We might compare the limitlessness of our good (the twelve baskets full of left-over bread and fish) to the principle of mathematics. Every person in the world could add, subtract, multiply and divide twenty-four hours a day, seven days a week, fifty-two weeks a year, and the principle of mathematics would not be lessened in any way. The principle of mathematics remains for all to continue to use.

This is true of God's good as well. Each human being can be totally healthy, yet God's wholeness in no way decreases. All can use and circulate God-substance whenever he or she desires to do so and the totality of God's supply remains. Every person on earth can express absolute love every moment of the day for the rest of his or her life, and all the love that has ever existed remains available. This is because all of our good begins within.

These are the steps used in Jesus' miracle model. He told us that everything he did, we could do, and even greater things. Then he showed us the way.

Thoughts For Contemplation Or Group Discussion

To follow Jesus' Miracle Model, You must:

1. Make a commitment to becoming the person you desire to be.
2. Have faith in your faith. Act as you would if you knew your prayer was answered *now*. Act as if it *is,* and it *will be*.
3. Give thanks in advance that your prayer is *now* answered.
4. Project your five physical senses into Spiritual substance. See, hear, taste, smell, and touch that which you desire. Experience it as an already accomplished fact in your life. You are creating your own spiritual pattern.
5. Deny the power of any belief that you will not be successful. Affirm that you are *now* a success!
6. Release your goal and let God bring it into being. Your job is *what*; God's job is *how*. Recognize that your miracles are limitless.
7. Relax. Turn away from the problem and set your vision on the spiritual goal or solution.
(Do you believe in *spiritual healing*? If so, how does it take place? What is your understanding of the *human ego*? What did Jesus do with his?

Give examples of *misusing* your spiritual thoughts and feelings. How must we deal with *unclean* thoughts and feelings? What is your understanding of the *Holy Trinity? What are the most effective ways you have found to accomplish these steps?*)

Miracle Referenced:

1. Supply – Feeding the five thousand (Matthew 14:13-23; Mark 6:30-46; Luke 9:10-17; John 6:1-16)

CHAPTER X

AS ABOVE, SO BELOW

"On earth as it is in heaven"

(Matthew 6:10).

Shortly after the miracle of the feeding of the five thousand, a strikingly similar story – the feeding of the four thousand – is told by the writers of Matthew and Mark (Matthew 15:32-39; Mark 8:1-9). Just prior to this event, however, several very important happenings took place that tie these two miracles of supply together in a surprisingly Spiritual way. Let us examine these events, as well as the feeding of the four thousand itself:

A Rocky Boat Ride

Following the feeding of the five thousand, Jesus remained behind with the crowd, sending his disciples on in a boat to Bethsaida. After their departure, he went up on a mountain to pray.

Evening came and the boat bearing the disciples was having a difficult time. Mark's story tells us that "...they were making headway painfully, for the wind was against them" (Mark 6:48). Matthew tells us the boat "...was many furlongs distant from the land, beaten by the waves; for the wind was against them" (Matthew 14:24). Jesus remained on shore.

Just before dawn he appeared to the disciples, walking on the sea. One would expect them to be jubilant at the sight of Jesus, but this was not the case. They were terrified, thinking they were seeing a ghost.

Sensing their fright, Jesus spoke to them saying, "Take heart, it is I; have no fear". And he entered the boat with them and the wind ceased (Mark 6:45-52; John 6:16-21; Matthew 14:22-36).

Have there been times in your life when you set out in your little boat (consciousness), attempting to sail against the wind without the conscious presence of the Christ? Most of us would probably answer in the affirmative. We may begin business ventures or relationships without considering their full spiritual impact.

We may drift into habits or lifestyles injurious to health or long-term happiness. We may allow reactive emotions to overwhelm us and temporarily overcome our good judgment.

They Say

At such times we inevitably find ourselves in an unstable mental and emotional state. We are truly in danger of becoming submerged in the waters of negation. The mind is fearful and physical challenges frequently follow such fear. When we attempt to sail a stormy sea, we are, as the Gospel writers described, beaten by waves and making headway painfully. In such a situation, the wind (that life force which propels us onward) is indeed, against us. In today's parlance, we might say, "The odds are stacked!"

Water symbolizes a number of things, one of which is that great mass of universal conforming thoughts often referred to as what "they say." Race mind is another name for it. The things they say may have been said for generations, but regularly a new group of "they sayers" speak up. Their words become known as peer pressure or that which is currently politically correct.

But just as things looked really bad for the disciples, before dawn when *they say* things are always darkest, the disciples recognized Jesus, and he told them, "Take heart, it is I; have no fear".

When we are in such a predicament – for example, we fear a disease which *they say* is incurable, or we fear for our future for *they say* hard times are inevitable, or we fear for the safety of ourselves and our loved ones for *they say*, "It's a jungle out there! You can't trust anybody" – at such a time, even the presence of the Christ walking beside us can be terrifying! But that Only Begotten Child of God placed at the very core of our beingness, the Christ, never fails us. Even through our cries and terror, that still, small voice persists until we hear, "Take heart, it is I; have no fear."

Peter Walks On The Water (Matthew 1:28-33)

Only the writer of the Gospel of Matthew elaborates on this event. He tells us that Peter, the disciple who symbolizes the spiritual faculty of faith in humankind, said to Jesus, "Lord, if it is you, bid me come to you on the water."

In other words, "Lord, I'm afraid of my shadow. I want to believe that I can overcome my fears, that I can overcome dire diagnoses, poverty prognostications, hopelessness – all of the things that *they*, the authority figures, tell me will happen. But Lord, I'm terrified! If it's *really you*, show me a sign! Bid me come to you. Help me overcome my belief in all the terrible things *they say* will happen."

And Jesus simply said to them, "Come." And we read that Peter got out of the boat and walked on the water toward Jesus.

All was well for Peter until he looked away from Jesus (the *solution*) and saw the wind (the *problem*). Then he was afraid. As he began to sink into the depths of the sea *(race mind)*, he cried in desperation, "Lord save me." And immediately, Jesus reached out his hand and caught him and said to him: "O man of little faith, why did you doubt?" And when they got into the boat, the wind ceased, and the disciples said to Jesus, "Truly you are the Son of God."

Have you ever faced such a predicament? I imagine most of us have. Things seemed hopeless, but as you turned to Spirit with all of your understanding, small as it might have seemed to be, you felt the presence of the Christ, and hope was restored: "Perhaps I can be healed!" "Perhaps I can prosper!" "Perhaps I am worthy of love!"

Then the wind blew, and the words *they say* echoed in your mind, and if you are like most of us, you began to sink back into the mire of universal negativity.

Fortunately, this is not the end of the story. The Christ of our being does not give up easily. The Christ reaches out a hand to our own Peter, our personal, God-given faculty of faith. The Christ holds us up until the wind ceases, until our consciousness of safety is restored, until we as human beings receive tangible evidence that we are not deserted, adrift on a windy, lonely sea.

Then that still small voice of Spirit speaks to us, "Why did you doubt?" and our faith is at least temporarily restored. Then our disciples, the spiritual faculties God has given to each human being, say in unison: "Truly you are the Child of God."

Stepping Out On The Water

It takes courage to step out onto that dark, windy sea and reach for the hand of the Christ. There are times when it may be easier to simply accept what *they say*, even if what *they say* is that we shall die.

In our morning paper I read an article quoting a prominent physician and church layman, chastising television evangelists who encourage faith healing. He stated:

The proper response of Christians to affliction is not to demand healing, but rather to witness to the world that through the grace of God, a Christian is able to accept affliction, trusting in the sovereignty of God.

I have no doubt that this gentleman's only desire is to be of help and comfort to those who are ill. Undoubtedly, faith does sustain when the time comes for life to depart this plane. But to ignore human potential for healing is to deny much on which Christianity is based. If healing of the human body and mind is not a part of the grace of God, we can only assume that Jesus was the greatest of frauds, for he denied the power of sickness in the human body, even unto death!

A lovely lady attended a class I taught each week. She had been a part of our church several years before. At first she sat quietly in the church courtyard where she meditated alone. There was a pensiveness about her that gradually changed to joy as winter turned to spring. She began to talk with some of the class members and finally, joined our morning prayer group. Eventually, she confided that during the year before, she had been diagnosed as having terminal cancer. She had an excellent doctor, she told us, though, because of lack of funds, she saw him less than she should. "They tell me that he knows by simply looking at a patient if he'll get well or not and when!"

"He's good," she went on. "But he's wrong this time" she added emphatically. "He doesn't know the things I've been taught. I haven't been to church for a while, but I never forgot the things I learned. And I'm back now. I'm meditating, I'm praying, and I know I've been healed!"

She certainly appeared to be healed. Had a stranger entered the classroom, she would surely have been among the least likely persons to be judged *terminally ill,* or even *ill* at all!

As the year progressed, she never missed a class or church service. Each week she was visibly stronger physically and spiritually. She felt good. She did her own housework. She was employed on a full-time basis. She took care of her elderly mother and a grandchild. She shopped. She laughed and enjoyed life.

One morning during class, she told us she had an appointment with her oncologist the day before our next meeting. "Won't he be surprised when he sees me!" she laughed, and we laughed with her, fully expecting a wonderful report.

The woman who came to class seven days later bore no resemblance to the one we had laughed with the week before. Her skin was sallow. She was bent and frail. "The doctor said I should get my affairs in order as soon as possible," she told us, then she added, "within a few weeks."

She was not in church or class the next week, nor any of the weeks that followed. From then on, I only saw her in a hospital bed, in obvious pain or drugged so heavily that communication was impossible.

Frank and I, as well as our church's Hospital Chaplain, visited her. We wanted to work with her individually on a regular basis, using spiritual and psychological techniques to help her overcome the condition. "No," she said. She was too tired. She was ready to go. "Just pray that it's easy," she whispered weakly. All that marvelous energy that had sustained her was gone, wiped out in one brief professional visit.

Good Intentions?

Surely the physician who told her to get her affairs in order had only good intentions. Nevertheless. I believe with all my heart that the effect of his words were the cause of her death. Her death certificate lists *carcinoma* as cause of death. Perhaps it should read, *terminal prognosis by excellent physician.*

Our friend had been walking on water (treading on race belief that cancer is inevitably fatal and a physician's word infallible). She walked on water with her hand outstretched to the Christ, and so long as she kept her eye on that goal, she thrived.

But the wind blew. The authority figure told her she was dying, and she took her eye off the solution and looked down at the murky, dismal waters of race mind. Then she sank into it. It was easier to obediently follow the authority figure's orders, like a good patient, than to continue to exercise her God-given faculty of faith.

Sam Revisited

Fortunately, it does not always end that way. In my first book, *LAWS OF LOVE* I told about *Sam*, (not his name) who entered the hospital for tests prior to surgery for a diagnosed malignancy.

Sam was a terrible patient. He refused to accept the diagnosis or to act as a proper hospitalized cancer patient was expected to act. He did not wear a gown, but wandered the halls in a business suit, visiting patients, telling jokes and discussing politics. When confronted with this unacceptable behavior, he insisted, "Oh, I'm not Sam Johnson. He's my brother. I'm here to visit him." Needless to say, Sam was a trial to the hospital staff

On election day, Sam checked himself out of the hospital to vote, assuring the bewildered surgeon that he would return immediately. They may still be waiting, because Sam, who recently turned ninety-one, has not yet returned to the hospital except to visit others. I can also report that he is the picture of robust good health with an enthusiasm for life matched by very few.

Let me tell you a little about Sam. I have known him all my life. Sam has faced challenges, but none of them overcame him, none took away his love and zest for living. Never have I known a person more interested in spiritual matters, nor one who more fully practices Truth principles in his personal life. I have never heard Sam complain nor speak an unkind word about anyone, even those who insist that his positive outlook on life is *strange!*

Nor is Sam's case an isolated one. It was dramatic. It took courage on the part of him and his family to stand up to such authority. But Sam and those like him have that courage, and they are beautiful examples for the rest of us.

These two stories might be considered coincidence. One might say that the woman from my class was only kidding herself, that she had simply psyched herself into believing a healing had taken place and was pushing beyond her limits. Sam's case might be called a misdiagnosis. This could be said, but I who have known them both personally do not believe it.

I could cite numerous cases of healings and non-healings. I have seen people who were literally *dying* to escape a situation that had become untenable for one reason or another. Others, like Sam, have such a love for life that nothing diminishes that desire to live.

The Pharisees Among Us

After Jesus and his disciples arrived safely on shore, a confrontation took place between them and the Pharisees. The Pharisees accused the disciples of transgressing the tradition of the elders by not washing their hands before they ate, an act which rendered an individual unfit to participate in worship with the rest of the Jewish community. Jesus responded by calling them *hypocrites* for adhering to the letter of the law and ignoring its spirit (Matthew 16:1-20; Mark 7:1-23).

You may recall that along with observing the letter and not the spirit of the law, a *Pharisee* metaphysically represents one *lacking in the understanding of Truth.* In this particular instance their complaint was Jesus' failure to follow *tradition.*

Few of us today would become overly concerned with another's hand-washing practices; nevertheless, the Pharisees did not disappear with the coming of Christianity. Though we may not realize it, each of us has

Pharisaical aspects within our own consciousness with which we contend. These inner *Pharisees* can appear at any time or place, often surprising us, for they are intent upon keeping the status quo, regardless of how limiting or outmoded it may have become.

My own personal *Pharisees* moved very reluctantly from my well-worn electric typewriter to the word processor, then to a computer that can do anything (I am told). They were comfortable with things as they were, and it took time and effort to learn to operate new machines.

Nor were my Pharisees limited to these devices.

I was even more surprised to find religious Pharisees within myself.

Both Frank and I were raised in traditional Christian churches that did not practice condemnation or over-emphasize rules, regulations or rituals. The time came, however, when we realized that we were giving a great deal of ourselves (teaching, directing choirs, serving on a variety of boards and committees, as well as financial support), while receiving very little spiritual nourishment in return. We can empty ourselves by giving with no replenishment for only so long before spiritual malnutrition sets in. You might say, we were like the hungry crowd that Jesus set out to feed.

Church was important to us for ourselves and our children. After exploring a number of churches and spiritual groups, we decided that Unity was the way of life that best met our needs and belief systems. We began visiting and eventually became members of a congregation. We gobbled that spiritual food in much the same way that the crowd ate the fish and bread provided by Jesus.

Does that sound like an instant happy ending? Ultimately yes, but not immediately.

So long as I visited *study groups* and kept Sunday sacred for *regular church,* examining new ideas presented no challenge to my personal *Pharisees*. But when we decided to spend Sunday mornings from eleven a.m. until noon at Unity, a change occurred. Pharisaical memories from my past swarmed over me. They did not discuss when or how I washed my hands as the Pharisees did with Jesus' disciples. That would have been too simple! What they did argue were the merits of every past religious ritual I had ever known, rituals and beliefs I never dreamed were still a part of my consciousness.

Nor were these *Pharisees* limited to mental and emotional visitors from within myself. My mother, whom I deeply loved and wanted very much to please, was sincerely concerned that my children were not receiving the benefit of sacraments that to her were essential. She never became comfortable with our decision, and during her lifetime, this was painful for me.

Other changes took place – most of them overwhelmingly constructive, but some brought a certain sadness. There were long-term friends with whom we no longer shared common interests because those common interests had centered around the social activities of a church we no longer attended.

It is important to be aware that when we make a commitment to radically change our lives, we must be prepared for the other changes that occur, for the *Pharisees* of tradition are not easily quieted.

Healing The Gentile Woman's Daughter

Immediately following Jesus' discussion with the Pharisees, he and his disciples went to the district of Tyre and Sidon, where they met a Gentile woman. Mark's version of the incident describes her as Greek, a Syrophoenician by birth (Matthew 16:21-28; Mark 7:24-30).

She beseeched Jesus, "Have mercy on me, O Lord, Son of David; my daughter is severely possessed by a demon." Jesus offered no response, and his disciples urged him to send her away, for she was not a Jew.

Jesus seemed to respond in kind: "I was sent only to the lost sheep of the house of Israel." But the woman persisted, "Lord help me." Jesus again declined. "It is not fair to take the children's bread and throw it to the dogs." The woman then replied, "Lord, even the dogs eat the crumbs that fall from their master's table. Jesus answered, "O woman, great is your faith! Be it done for you as you desire." And we read that her daughter was healed instantly.

If we look at this episode on the literal level alone, we cannot fail to observe a bit of racial/religious intolerance, not only on the part of the disciples, but from Jesus, as well. The Gentile woman was considered *unclean* to the faithful Jew, just as a dog was considered unclean.

Jesus' response, "It is not fair to take the children's bread and throw it to the dogs," could not have been misunderstood. Had he been running for public office today, he would have had a great deal of explaining to do regarding such a statement!

Nor was its meaning lost on the woman. She recognized that she was being compared to a *dog*. Her response that "...even the dogs eat the crumbs that fall from their master's table" shows that she was fully aware of how she was regarded by the group.

The fact that Jesus might have experienced prejudice may be disturbing to some, though this does appear to be an isolated incident. Most actions and parables do not show this side of Jesus.

He was, however, a product of a society steeped in tradition. Just as certain unacceptable traditions in our country went unquestioned by many good people for years, it may be that at this time in his life, Jesus was so deeply concerned with the Spiritual wellbeing of his own people (Israel) that social injustices were not uppermost in his mind. If we judge this on a literal level, the important thing to note is that the human being, Jesus, was capable of changing his point of view.

This Gentile woman, fully recognizing how she was considered by Jesus and his followers, had enough faith and love for her daughter to meet the situation, boldly stand up to it and insistently seek help. Jesus was obviously impressed by her faith and commitment, and her daughter was healed.

The Personal Ego

Now let's look at this incident from the metaphysical point of view.

Tyre and Sidon, cities on the eastern coast of the Mediterranean Sea, were Gentile areas. The *King of Tyre* literally refers to the *personal, unilllumined* human ego, the *ruling power in the five-sense person. Syrophoenlcians* refer to natives of Phoenicia when it was a part of the Roman province of Syria. Clearly, the woman was Gentile.

We have seen before that a *Jew* refers to *Spiritualized thoughts and feelings,* or at least *those thoughts and feelings that are seeking Spirit. A Gentile* (all nations and peoples not of Israelite origin and faith) refers to *worldly thoughts* – thoughts pertaining to the *physical,* or *thoughts that function through the senses.* Metaphysically, this woman represented a human, physical challenge.

Let us now examine this incident, not as an event taking place outside, but as an internal event within ourselves. We know that our indwelling Christ (represented by Jesus) always hears and answers us; nevertheless, there are times when we're like the importunate widow in Jesus' parable (Luke 18:1-8). We have not been able to realize our oneness with this inner Source; thus, we feel unclean or unworthy, and our request may *seem* to be ignored and go unanswered. If we persist, as did this Gentile woman and the importunate widow, contact is inevitably made.

Women

Women refer to the *feeling nature. Jewish women* refer to *feelings* that are *seeking Spirit.* A *gentile woman* refers to *feelings or emotions on a human level.* Many of these feelings and emotions are wonderful. Without them, we could not enjoy life on earth, or even exist at all. They have their origin in Spirit, and are designed to eventually bring about that at-one-ment of body, mind/soul and Spirit.

Nevertheless, there are times when these God-given feelings have produced secondary emotions (the Gentile woman's daughter) that may appear to have a demon. A very obvious example might be *mother-love*. This form of love is essential to the preservation of the human species, and it is beautiful. Mother-love can, however, turn into *smother-love,* and when it does, its possessor could easily be described as having a demon.

Nor should the *demon* of the gentile woman's daughter be limited to women alone. *Mother/smother* love has a certain ring to it, yet all true feelings can be misinterpreted and misapplied as easily by men as by women.

The desire to procreate was placed in all of God's earthly creation, yet it can be misused and lead to promiscuity. The desire to be successful in life is a God-inspired goal, yet its priorities may become confused and *workaholism* may result. Peace of mind is a desire for which all of us yearn, yet many seek it through chemicals, rather than prayer and meditation.

The Gentile woman's daughter represents a feeling or emotion that has risen up from within the human soul and needs to be healed. We do not know the nature of the demon possessing this offspring (daughter), yet we do know that this woman recognized it for what it was, and courageously sought healing from Jesus.

Not only did she seek healing; she persisted until she made contact with the Christ; then her faith brought that healing into being.

If we want to make a miracle, we must be willing to do the same. We must bring our demon-possessed offspring, those misinterpretations of our good, to the Christ of our being to be cleansed and made whole.

Meditation

When Jesus left that area and went to the Sea of Galilee, he and his disciples went up on a mountain. Again great crowds came to him, bringing their lame, maimed, blind, dumb and those with other afflictions, and laid them at his feet. Jesus healed them and the people were amazed when they saw the dumb speaking, the maimed made whole, the lame walking and the blind seeing, and they glorified the God of Israel (Matthew 15:29-31).

Jesus understood the importance of maintaining the body, mind/soul/spirit balance; thus, prayer and meditation were integral parts of his life. It must be the same for us as well. When we gather our spiritual faculties (disciples) together and move to a consciousness of prayer and meditation (a mountain), we do not automatically find peace. Frequently we find quite the opposite!

Oftentimes, as noted before, great crowds of thoughts and feelings rush in on us, bringing with them their crippled and maimed aspects, those parts of us which are unable to see clearly or speak the Truth. It is during such a time that the Christ of our being heals these human afflictions. These are the very ones that need the touch of the healing Christ.

A Gentile Man

As Jesus and his disciples moved on through the Gentile area of Decapolis, a man who was deaf and had a speech impediment was brought to them. Jesus took him away from the crowd and, in private, healed him by placing his fingers in his ears and touching his tongue with spittle, then saying "Ephatha," meaning, "Be opened." And all were astonished at this healing (Mark 7:31-37).

Decapolis, a Roman district, was partly in Syria and partly in Palestine. Since this was a *male Gentile,* he represents *thoughts* (as opposed to feelings) *of a human nature,* possibly even *confused thoughts,* since the area in which he lived was in both Jewish and Gentile territory. He may have been confused as to what in life is important, the body or the Spirit. If only Spirit is important, then why should he desire to hear and speak. But if only the body has value, how could he even hope for a healing to take place?

Note that the first thing Jesus did was to take the man away from the crowd, and heal him privately. When we need a healing of body, mind or affairs, we must remove ourselves from the crowd of confused thoughts and feelings that swarm about us.

Syria, a portion of Decapolis, refers to *intellect and intellectual pride.* But the district in which the man lived was not totally in Syria. He was in the area containing both Syria and Palestine or Israel. He was *coming from the* intellect, but also from the deep yearning of Spirit to be healed, to be able to hear and understand and to speak and be truly understood.

Recognizing this intellectual need, we can see why it was necessary that Jesus take some kind of outer action, in this instance placing his fingers in the man's ears and touching his tongue with spittle. Surely it was not for Jesus' benefit that this placebo effect was offered. Jesus understood that faith was the power that healed, yet he also knew that it was essential for the person seeking healing to have that faith.

The intellect demands proof. The intellect cannot believe that faith alone is sufficient to heal. It insists that cures come about through some (to it) rational and logical manner visible to the human eye. Spittle was believed by the people of that day to have curative powers; thus, Jesus gave this man that which his intellect demanded in order that he receive the healing.

On an even deeper level, however, have there not been times in your own life when you have experienced confused, perhaps even unclean thinking, the inability to hear and understand the voice of Spirit within, or to express yourself in prayer to God?

Confused, Unclean Thinking

And what of those times when your speech impediment has reached the point that you use psychological or clinical denial (as opposed to spiritual denial) to lie to yourself? This is a common human practice; "I don't have an alcohol problem. Why, I can stop drinking anytime!" or "I know I'm a little overweight. It runs in my family. There's nothing I can do about it", or "I know I spend too much time (or not enough time) at the office, but that's just the way I am." Surely we are all familiar with such inner dialogue.

Without the ability to trust and understand ourselves, spiritually and intellectually, we are *neither fish nor fowl*. We are like prisoners in an alien land.

It is possible that this Gentile man who lived in an area partly of Spirit and partly of the intellect could represent the confusion of the religious absolutist who insists that only Spirit is valid or even exists at all, not comprehending that we are threefold beings – body, mind/soul and Spirit. We are, indeed, a *Holy Trinity which* must be maintained and integrated in balance.

But the compassionate Christ heals all conditions, for nothing we can need or desire is beneath His caring, nor is anything hidden from Him.

A Banquet For Four Thousand

In the Gospel of Mark the feeding of the four thousand follows the healing of the Gentile woman and man. Mark's and Matthew's version of this supply miracle are almost identical. This is Matthew's version (Matthew 15:32-38):

> Then Jesus called his disciples to him and said, "I have compassion on the crowd, because they have been with me now three days, and have nothing to eat; and I am unwilling to send them away hungry, lest they faint on the way." And the disciples said to him, "Where are we to get bread enough in the desert to feed so great a crowd?" and Jesus said to them, "How many loaves have

you?" They said, "Seven, and a few small fish." And commanding the crowd to sit down on the ground, he took the seven loaves and the fish, and having given thanks he broke them and gave them to the disciples, and the disciples gave them to the crowds, and they all ate and were satisfied; and they took up seven baskets full of broken pieces left over. Those who ate were four thousand men, besides women and children.

The same steps are taken in this miracle that Jesus took to feed the five thousand. The spiritual pattern had been completed; now it was time to reap the physical harvest.

Jesus had faith in his God-given ability to provide food with only a small amount of bread and fish available. Not for one moment did he hesitate or doubt that this would take place; thus, he made a commitment to do so. (He had compassion on the crowd and would not send them away hungry.)

Meditation and relaxation were practiced. ("He called his disciples to him" and told the crowd to "sit down on the ground.") Jesus then activated the power of the imagination and the word. (The *seven* loaves represent the *five* physical senses, plus the *two* words – the ability to affirm and deny.) "A few small fish" refers to ideas.

By "breaking" the bread (imagination, plus affirmation and denial) and fish (ideas), Jesus activated the power which brings our desire into physical manifestation. When we accept inspiration from Spirit and combine it with the power of our imagination, using affirmations and denials, our prayer is answered and our demonstration is made right here on earth.

As always, Jesus completed his miracle-making by giving thanks in advance for that which was to be.

Though the stories of the feeding of the five and four thousand are so similar one might almost think they are the same story, there are some obvious differences: first, the location; second, the length of time the crowd had been with Jesus; and last and perhaps most important, the difference in the amount of food left over after everyone had eaten and was satisfied.

Differences

Note the location.

The feeding of the five thousand takes place in *his own country* according to Matthew and Mark (Matthew 15:29; Mark 7:31) in Bethsaida according to Luke (Luke 9:10), in Galilee according to John (John 6:1). Each of these accounts refers to Galilee, since Nazareth, the boyhood home of Jesus was in Galilee, as was Bethsaida. Galilee was also on Jewish soil. Since *Jews* represent *thoughts and feelings seeking Spirit, Jewish territory*, from a metaphysical standpoint, refers to a *spiritual state of consciousness*.

The feeding of the *four thousand*, according to both Matthew and Mark, took place in *Gentile territory*. This refers to a *human or physical state of mind*.

In the story of the feeding of the five thousand, the people had been with Jesus for *one day*. In the feeding of the four thousand, the crowd had been with Jesus for *three days*.

Metaphysically, the number *one* refers to *God*, for God is One. "Hear, O Israel: The Lord our God is one.." (Deuteronomy 6:4). *Three* is the number of *humankind – body mind/soul and Spirit*.

In the story of the feeding of the five thousand all ate and were satisfied, and twelve baskets of food were left over. In the feeding of the four thousand all ate and were satisfied, and seven baskets were left.

Twelve is the number of *spiritual completion*. *Seven* is the number of *human completion*.

When we closely examine these two miracles, using the secret code with which the Hebrews were so familiar, we find a very important meaning. In the feeding of the four thousand we are told that not only are our spiritual needs important to the Christ of our being and worthy of total and absolute satisfaction, but our *human, physical needs* are equally important and worthy of satisfaction as well.

And our needs are not met in some bare, minimal fashion. They are *lavishly* met. We are designed to have vibrant health of body, mind and emotions. We are intended to have abundant prosperity. We are worthy of being deeply loved and returning that love in full. This is God's plan for each one of us. Nothing less is good enough for God's child!

And God's provision for us is never depleted; seven baskets of bread and fish (substance and ideas – wholeness on the physical plane) remain after all have *eaten* their fill.

From the beginning of time, there have been those who taught that the human body is a thing to be looked down upon, to be mortified, existing only as the result of some dreadful *original sin* into which humankind fell. Even certain metaphysical groups of today teach a kind of *good Spirit, bad body* philosophy.

This was not the teaching of Jesus. He taught and demonstrated that we are a unity composed of body, mind/soul and Spirit, all of which are equally important. The goal is not to eliminate one or two, but to *integrate the three*. This is what Jesus did. Was this not what he was saying when he prayed, "Thy kingdom come. Thy will be done, on earth as it is in heaven" (Matthew 6:10).

We are designed to have vibrant good health of body, mind and emotions. We are intended to have abundant prosperity. We are worthy of being deeply loved and returning that love in full. This is God's plan for each one of us. Nothing less is good enough for God's child!

And God's provision for us is never depleted; seven baskets of bread and fish (substance and ideas) remain after all have "eaten" their fill.

The Miracle Model Again

The same steps apply in bringing about our earthly good as our spiritual good, and they are the same steps that Jesus used in his "Miracle Model."

We must, first of all, relax and recognize God as the Source of all our supply. We then make a commitment to do our part in bringing that supply, whatever it might be, into physical manifestation. We work to enhance our faith, recognizing that faith is the power that makes miracles. We give thanks that the answer to our prayer exists for us now and is ours in accomplished fact. We use our five physical senses in the "imaging" process, placing ourselves in the midst of our completed goal and enjoying it! We deny the power of any belief or feeling that this goal cannot be achieved by and for us, and affirm that it is now in the process of coming into actual being. The final step is to release that prayer, allowing God to bring it into being in God's own way.

You were created to enjoy life to the fullest and claim your good, to assist others in doing the same, and to daily give thanks for the marvelous experience of life on earth. Never forget that it is God's will that you be healthy, happy, prosperous, loved, loving, and successful in every way. You are God's greatest miracle, and you were designed to make a miracle too!

Thoughts For Contemplation Or Group Discussion:

1. When we are afraid and surrounded by race beliefs and all the things that "they say" will happen, the Christ of our being is right beside us, holding out a hand to us, strengthening our faith, enabling us to stay on top of the situation, whatever it might be. We must keep an eye on the solution, not the problem!
2. We have "Pharisees" within us that are fearful and reluctant of "letting go" of old ways. There are also people close to us who wish to retain the "status quo," and cannot understand why we wish to change.

3. Some of the Gentile women within us (worthy human feelings) have given birth to misinterpretations of what our true desires are. When this takes place, these "offspring" concepts must be healed of their "demons" by our indwelling Christ.
4. We have "Gentile men" (confused human thoughts) within our consciousness that do not hear and understand and do not speak that which is Spiritually True. Their hearing and speech impediments must be healed.
5. Our human needs are worthy of satisfaction. When we seek them spiritually, there is enough for all, with an infinity left over.
6. We human beings are composed of body, mind/soul and Spirit. All aspects of this "trinity" are holy and blessed by God!
(Do metaphysical interpretations make understanding clearer? Easier? Discuss as it applies to the examples given above.)

Inspired Thoughts On Human Life

1. "These things I have spoken to you, that my joy may be in you, and that your joy may be full" – Jesus (John 15:11).

2. "In thinking of ourselves, we must not separate Spirit, soul and body, but rather hold all as one, if we would be strong and powerful" – Emilie Cady LESS0NS IN TRUTH, p. 25).
3. "The doctrine of the trinity is often a stumbling block, because we find it difficult to understand how three persons can be one. Three persons cannot be one, and theology will always be a mystery until theologians become metaphysicians." – Charles Fillmore *Revealing Word,* p. 199).
4. "We live in deeds, not years: in thoughts, not breaths; in feelings, not in figures on a dial. We should count time by heart-throbs. He most lives who thinks most, feels the noblest, acts the best." Bailey.
5. "This also, that I live, I consider a gift of God." Ovid.

Miracles Referenced:

1. Nature – Walking on water – (Matt. 14:22-36; Mark 6:45-52); (John 6:15-21)
2. Healing – Canaanite woman's daughter – (Matt. 15:21-29)
3. Syrophoenician woman's daughter (Mark 7:25-30)
4. Healings – Crowd of maimed, blind, dumb and others (Mathew-15:29-31) Deaf man with speech impediment (Mark 7:31-37)

5. Supply – Feeding the five thousand – (Matt. 14:13-21; Mark 6:30-44; Luke 9:10-17; John 6:1-13)
6. Supply – Feeding the four thousand – (Matthew 15:32-39: Mark 8:1-10)

www.ingramcontent.com/pod-product-compliance
Lightning Source LLC
Chambersburg PA
CBHW061633040426
42446CB00010B/1391